Thomas Proctor

Presentation of the battle flags of the Oneida County regiments to the Oneida Historical Society, Utica, N.Y

Thomas Proctor

Presentation of the battle flags of the Oneida County regiments to the Oneida Historical Society, Utica, N.Y

ISBN/EAN: 9783337107543

Hergestellt in Europa, USA, Kanada, Australien, Japan

Cover: Foto ©ninafisch / pixelio.de

Weitere Bücher finden Sie auf www.hansebooks.com

Presentation of the...

..Battle Flags..

OF THE

Oneida County Regiments

TO THE

Oneida Historical Society,

...UTICA, N. Y...

TO MY COMRADES of the Grand Army of the Republic the following account of the presentation of the Battle Flags of the Oneida County Regiments, together with General N. M. Curtis' lecture on the Capture of Fort Fisher, is respectfully dedicated.

It is largely copied from the Utica Daily Newspapers—the Observer, the Herald and the Press.

THOMAS R. PROCTOR,
Post Reynolds, G. A. R.

MUNSON-WILLIAMS MEMORIAL.
Home of the Battle Flags of the Oneida County Regiments.

To the Oneida Historical Society:

On the occasion of its assuming the custody of the old flags of the Oneida County Regiments.

    Guard well and ever watchful be,
    So every coming age may see,
    That in the cause of liberty,
     They were never trailed in dust.
    They gained the freedom for a race,
    They saved the nation from disgrace,
    With loving hands we proudly place
     Into thy charge this sacred trust.

    Oft midst the shriek of shot and shell,
    Oft on the field where patriots fell,
    With love that treason could not quell,
     These banners, brave men proudly bore.
    Flags of the Union strong and great,
    'Tis not surrender that we make,
    But midst the jewels of the State,
     In splendor shine forever more.

        R. D. S. MORTIMER, Brookfield, Mass.

1st Lieut., Co. C., 2d N. Y. H. A.

[From *Utica Morning Herald*, Dec. 14, 1897.]

 THE OLD FLAGS.

As an appropriate prelude to the ceremonies marking the presentation to the Oneida Historical Society of the old flags, carried in the war for the Union by Oneida County regiments, the Herald prints this morning letters from veterans to whom the tattered flags and their perpetual care are especially dear. One writer only expresses regret at the disposition made of these relics of patriotic association—Sergeant Hiram H. Gibbs, of Syracuse, Company H, 14th N. Y. Volunteers. And this dissident writes, we think, under misapprehension. Care of the flags, not their seclusion from sight of "the boys" who followed them, is the controlling thought in placing them in a safe place, in charge of an Association that will cherish and preserve them for what they are—trust bequests of men who are drawing near "the eternal camping ground" to which they can not take these sacred relics. The meeting there will be the happier for the knowledge that the old flags are daily an object lesson in patriotism, in the community where they were made, and to which they were returned with honor.

These letters from veterans will be welcome to all comrades, and to the general public.

FROM CAPTAIN H. R. LAHEE.

The flags of the Fourteenth never disgraced Oneida county or Lewis county on the battlefield. Take good care of the flags. We will soon be gone, but let the old flags remain forever.

H. R. LAHEE, Appleton, Wis.
Captain Co. I, 14th N. Y. Vols.

FROM THOMAS J TIMMONS.

The happiest days of my life, while a thoughtless, fearless, beardless young man, I spent following the flag of the Fourteenth Regiment. Sometimes hungry, wet and cold, everything looked dark, yet under the leadership of our gallant Colonel McQuade we never failed to come to the front at the proper time and in our proper place.

How proud he was of his flags, and how proud he was of his regiment. God bless his ashes.

The Oneida Historical Society can well be proud of the old flags, as they were always at the front when called upon to be there.

THOMAS J. TIMMONS, Yonkers.
Co. H, 14th N. Y. Vols.

FROM SERGEANT H. H. GIBBS.

It is with deep regret and sorrow that I now learn that the flags of the Fourteenth Regiment. N. Y. S. Vols. are to be turned over to the Oneida Historical Society. In May, 1861, I was a beardless boy of 17 years, and hearing of Fort Sumter falling into the hands of our southern brethren, my blood boiled within me, and one morning I left my country home and went to Syracuse to enlist. After waiting a little time on the streets, not really knowing where to go, some boys about my age came up to me and asked me if I wanted to enlist. I told them I did, and they asked me to enlist in their company, which I did. This proved to be Captain Thompson's company H of Syracuse, which went to make up the 14th N. Y., Colonel James McQuade's Utica regiment. We were mustered into the United States service in Albany, May 17, 1861, and from this time we began the soldier's life in earnest. The colors of a regiment are its pride. The old Fourteenth was always proud of its flags. The ladies of Utica gave us a beautiful silk flag and we were very anxious to return it, although tattered and torn, I can remember how we marched through the streets of Albany as an escort to the remains of Colonel Ellsworth, who had fallen at the hands of the traitor Jackson, for tearing down the rebel flag. We were proud of our flag, and we followed it to the capital of our nation, and as we stacked arms in the yard of the White House, and made our coffee I remember our now lamented President Lincoln and his wife coming out on the veranda. How the boys cheered them. For two long years we followed the flags through many a hard fought battle, and never were they taken from us. Many precious lives went out in their defense and many a poor soldier was crippled for life. I remember when my eyes looked upon them for the first time in thirty years the tears came trickling down my face. I took those battle scarred folds in my hand, I pressed them to my lips, and oh, the thoughts of other days came rushing through my memory. I thought of the brave men that stood by it in the dark days. There was that brave and gallant Colonel McQuade, who did not know fear, and after a few years of a citizen's life has gone to his reward. There was Lieutenant Colonel Skillin, who gave up his life at Gaines Mills. A braver man never honored the Union cause. There was that daring Major Davies, who did his duty nobly and is sleeping in a soldier's grave. There were many of the rank and file of the regiment that gave life and limb to honor the flag and preserve our nation. As these recollections come over me the old time patriotism burns anew in my breast. Now that the flags are to be turned over into other hands, the thought that perhaps my eyes may never look upon them again brings sorrow to my heart. I hope to meet all of the boys on the eternal camping ground.

HIRAM H. GIBBS, Syracuse.
Sergeant Co. H, 14th N. Y. Vols.

FROM A MEMBER OF COMPANY E.

The old flag, the dear old flag, although tattered and torn and bullet pierced, we love it still, for it brings back memories of thirty-five and thirty-six years ago, of the camp and the dress parade, general inspections and long marches by day and by night, the hard contested battles and of comrades that are sleeping far away from home.

MEMBER COMPANY E.
14th N. Y. Vols.

FROM PRIVATE JOHN E. EVANS.

I have not seen the flags of the old Fourteenth in thirty-four years, but it seems to me that I see them still. I can recollect well when they were presented to us. It was in the Park at New York city, by a delegation of citizens from Utica. Our flags were the first that were carried on the streets of Baltimore, after the assault made on the 6th Massachusetts. They were also saluted by "Old Abe" as we passed the White House door on our way to the camp on the White House grounds. On our advance up the Peninsula they were the first flags seen by the First Georgia Cavalry at Howard's Mills, where we had a skirmish, The day following, at Yorktown, they were the first Union flags seen by Magruder's army. They were the colors that came to the assistance of the 2d Maine and the 44th N. Y. at Hanover Court House. They were the flags that came to the relief of the 1st Pennsylvania Bucktails at Beaver Dam Creek, when they were badly pressed by D. H. Hill's troops. At Gaines Mills our flags were on the left flank with Companies B and I, when they were carried in three distinct charges and protected by the boys of two companies. Colonel McQuade and Major Davies were both with us at this point. At Malvern Hill three rebel regiments charged on us and tried to capture our flags, but we saved them and returned them to Utica at the end of two years. They were the first flags seen by Uticans that had been to the war.

JOHN E. EVANS, Winfield, Kan.
Private Co. B, 14th N. Y.

FROM A. B. CLEVELAND.

That once beautiful old glory, the pride of a thousand loyal hearted, I won't say boys in blue, nor bluecoats, but boys in gray. We did not have blue coats when this flag was new to us. We wore the gray, not the gray of the south, but of this old Empire State. Note the contrast of one of New York State's most notable of fighting regiments, carrying as beautiful a stand of colors as it was the good fortune of any regiment to possess, made of the finest of silk, and presented to the regiment by the loyal ladies of this beautiful Mohawk city, to be carried by their brave boys, clad in suits that even Governor Morgan and Senator Conkling were ashamed of. Then, too, it now bears a contrast with many others in appearance, showing how manfully it was kept before the eyes of the enemy, in the great struggle for the perpetuation of our great and glorious Union.

I can only say furthermore, that I having been only a musician, it was not my fortune to keep very close to the flag during battle, as I was, at other duties. I was always found to be one to rally around the dear old flag, when the drum was beating calling together the survivors of each battle the regiment was engaged in. And I loved to behold its beautiful blue field, the stars and stripes, though tattered and torn, as it emerged from the conflict. All hail to its glorious achievements, and may it long be preserved in the archives of the Oneida County Historical Association as a momento of the valor of its supporters and followers.

ANSON B. CLEVELAND, Utica.
Musician, Co. I, 26th N. Y. Vols.

FROM LIEUTENANT W. H. SANFORD.

The placing of the old flags of the Oneida County Regiments in the care of the Oneida County Historical Society is, I think, very appropriate.

The dear old flags; what a flood of memory is brought to mind, when the dear old flag is mentioned.

Our flag was presented to the regiment by the ladies of Utica in the early days of 1861. It was a very handsome one. The regiment felt proud of their flag.

I can see it now as it waved on the many bloody battlefields of the regiment during its two years' service. I can see it gracefully waved in regulation salute as little Mac and our martyred president, the noble Abraham Lincoln, reviewed the army, soon after the battle of Antietam.

After two years of faithful service we returned as a regiment, brought back the old flag unsullied, badly torn and shredded by shot and shell.

After our discharge many of us re-entered the service, and served till the close of the war, but I venture to say there is nothing that will quicken the pulse and brighten the eye of the comrades of the 26th Regiment like the mention of that old flag.

W. H. SANFORD, Clinton, N. Y.
1st. Lieut. Co. F., 26th N. Y. Vols.

FROM COLONEL RUFUS DAGGETT.

The survivors of the 117th Regiment will place the flag presented by the ladies of Utica in the case provided for it by Comrade T. R. Proctor at the Historical Building. This flag was carried through ten engagements, and was under almost constant fire through two sieges, that of Fort Wagner at Charleston Harbor, S. C., and Petersburg, Va. Its silk is tattered and torn, the staff was twice broken by shot or shell. After the battle at Drury's Bluff an inspection of the flags was made. The silk of this one was found pierced in several places, and the staff broken. Color Sergeant William E Pease (now dead) was severely wounded while gallantly holding it to the front. Others of the color guards, whose names I do not now recall, were wounded. The 117th was very proud of its regimental flag and never once forgot the written injunction given it by the donors, a copy of which will be deposited with the flag. On the return of the regiment this flag was in charge of Corporal E. S. Foskett, now a resident of this city. At the final muster out of the 117th by its action I became the proud possessor of it, and thirty-two years it has been in my family. Its further history can be read from the case in the Historical Building.

RUFUS DAGGETT, Utica.
Col. 117th N. Y. Vols.

FROM LIEUTENANT-COLONEL MEYERS.

It is gratifying to know that a suitable place has been provided by the Historical Society for the care and preservation of the old flags and other relics of Oneida County organizations that participated in the civil war. A place, not only of safety, but where they will be exposed to view and, as trust, inspire many American boys with a greater and better appreciation of that great struggle.

The veterans who so jealously watched over and defended these flags will derive a peculiar satisfaction in paying occasional visits to the weather beaten and tattered remnants of our colors, which, though so often enveloped in the smoke of battle, were never relinquished. The incidents in the history of the colors of the 117th N. Y. Vols. are indellibly recorded with bullets and shells on the silken folds and staff. Long after the last survivor has ceased to answer roll call these mute witnesses will continue to teach young American boys the awful fury and the perils of battle, which perhaps may lead them to discover in history how many of our comrades laid down their lives to save an untarnished flag and a country for them as a rich heritage.

Lieut. Col. F. X. MYERS.
Brev. Col. U. S. A.

Tribute of Company C.

Five and thirty years ago the patriotic ladies of the city of Utica and the great county of Oneida presented to the Fourth Oneida Regiment a beautiful silken flag, fashioned by their fair hands. It was presented to that band of brave men, not only as an emblem and symbol of our national integrity and existence, but as a token of their love and measure of devotion to the great cause of American liberty, which is the crowning glory of American citizenship.

It was borne by brave hearts, strong and willing hands through many a field of carnage and bloodshed, from your capital city to the burning sands of Morris Island, the stronghold of treason and rebellion. Then for many a long and dreary day before the impregnable walls of Petersburg; then through snow and sleet down the storm ridden Atlantic coast, to be first among many of the glorious stars and stripes to be planted in triumph upon the fortress of Fort Fisher.

Your course is marked by the bodies of many brave men strewn along your pathway, whose deeds and sacrifices will live in the history of our country long after your tattered silken folds shall have passed into dust and oblivion.

Our love for you passeth the love of woman and all other earthly things, aye—even the love of God.

The fires of patriotism kindled by our forefathers upon the altar of their country burn with undiminished brightness; that forms a bulwark of millions of American freemen that stand ready to respond to the bugle call for the defense of this emblem of the highest type of American freedom.

Our enfeebled limbs and trembling hands admonish us that we can no longer protect and care for you with our old time strength and vigor, and we consign your sacred folds to the outstretched hands waiting to receive you, with implicit faith and trust in their guardianship. Good bye, old flag, good bye.

From Color Sergeant Ernst.

I am happy to think that the flags are to be given to the Oneida Historical Society to be kept safe for future generations. I perhaps have as much interest in their safe keeping as any one of my comrades in the regiment. In the engagement September 29, 1864, on Chapin's Farm, at Fort Gilmore, our State banner was abandoned and left in front of the fort. The corporal who was carrying it became wounded in the wrist, and then our line gave way and retreated, leaving the colors. I did not like the idea of retreating, but when I saw it was useless to resist under that horrible firing, I turned about, and in the same row in the cornfield, went back to the edge of the field, where I found General Foster. He asked me where I was going, and I told him to the rear, that I couldn't take the fort alone. He told me to stay there with him to help rally the colored troops which were ordered up. I got in their ranks and told them we would take the fort yet. A six footer at my right said it was always the way, when the white troops were repulsed, the colored troops had to take the brunt of it. Just about that time a shell from the right took part of his face off, and why I was not hit I never could conceive. The colored troops gave way before they reached the line from where our boys retreated. Just then I noticed a stand of colors, and went and got them. When I got to the rear I found our boys in the road. I went up to the color sergeant and asked him if he was short of colors and he said he was, so I turned them over. This is how the flag was abandoned and restored again to its proper place, and we as comrades of the 117th can rejoice that we didn't return to Oneida County minus one of our flags.

John D. Ernst, Rome, N. Y.

Color Sergeant 117th N. Y. Vols.

From Sergeant J. B. Wicks.

Every member of the 117th is deeply interested in anything pertaining to the old regimental flags. We are all present wherever they are. They came to us clean as we began our service in 1862. For three years in the fie d they were the rallying centre of the regiment. At Charleston, Chapin's Farm, Drury's Bluff and Fort Fisher they had their greater consecration, and in its uplifting every man of the regiment was born again. I recall their forward charge at Drury's Bluff and Chapin's Farm. At Fort Fisher they were in the dash for that shell ,torn parapet, and waved like a cheer in the shout of victory five hours later.

From Fisher on to Raleigh they were borne in the march with Sherman and at the "muster out" we brought them back to the old home, tattered and torn, but new and blessed, in every wide rent and stain—in every faded stripe and star. The colors of the old regiment embody three years of marching, fighting, enduring. They mean life, alive and alert, in holy things.

With their fellow flags they will make the Munson-Williams Memorial Building our county shrine of richest soldier hope and memory.

J. B. WICKS, Paris, N. Y.
Sergeant Co. G 117th N. Y. Vols.

FROM PERRY B. MILLER.

Early in the spring of 1864 I was detailed as one of the color guard and remained with the colors until the close of the war. The flags were badly shattered by the enemy in several engagements, but we never for a moment thought that we would surrender them. We had made a solemn promise to the donors of the State flag that we would return it to Oneida County without the slightest disgrace. I will not attempt to mention the happenings in the many engagements until at Fort Fisher our flags, both National and State, were badly riddled. The National flagstaff was hit five times in this engagement, twice broken by bullets. We held it up while Fred Boden tied it together. The State flag was once broken and tied by John B. Jones.'

When the fort was surrendered Boden said: "Well, boys, we have got our flags but they are a little the worse for wear and only one of our members killed."

We buried him the next day. He had five bullet holes through his breast.

PERRY B. MILLER, Camden.
Co. B, 117th N. Y. Vols.

FROM CORPORAL HENRY H. MILLER.

The veterans of Oneida County have reason to be thankful to the Oneida Historical Society, and especially to Mr. Proctor, for the splendid arrangements they have made for preserving the flags of the Oneida County regiments. We all love and revere the old tattered flags that were with us in our marches by day and night, in camp and on battlefield. Many a comrade willingly sacrificed his life in defense of those flags and to preserve this beautiful land of ours. And now they are likely to be preserved to coming generations and in years to come, when the old veterans shall be held in reverent yet mystic memory, if these cases could be unsealed and flags unfurled, what thrilling tales they could tell to one who could interpret their language of daring and heroic deeds, of Antietam, Gettysburg, the Wilderness, Cold Harbor, Petersburg, Chapin's Farm, Fort Fisher and others, for they were there. If not in this way, I am sure in some way they will be an inspiration to the patriotic devotion and love of country to those that shall come after us.

HENRY H. MILLER, Clinton, N. Y.
Corporal Co. K, 117th N. Y. Vols.

FROM CORPORAL S. NELSON.

I look back to the stirring times of '61 to '65, when at the age of nineteen I gave my services as a volunteer in Co. F. 117th N. Y. Vols., holding the office of corporal, and taking part with the regiment in building fortifications to make sure defense of our national capital during the winter of '62, and served until the close of the war. It was in the month of November, 1862, that the ladies of Utica presented the regiment with a beautiful silk banner, which was carried throughout by the regiment and was brought home in tatters at the close, having been pierced many times by bullets from the country's foes. I am amongst the least worthy of the boys who composed the regiment, but I tried to fulfill my part of duty as health and opportunity permitted. The war records show how well the regiment performed its part.

S. NELSON, Oriskany.
Corporal Co. F, 117th N. Y. Vols.

FROM SERGEANT MARRIOTT.

Nothing appears more appropriate than to speak of the regiment's weary march from Fort Fisher to Wilmington. It was on February 22d, (Washington's birthday,) that the 117th, after days of weary tramping and experiencing all sorts of privations, entered that city. The old colors, soiled and tattered, were now unfurled and the boys tried to cheer. But at the sight of the blessed old flags, torn into shreds, our boys were overcome with sorrow, and there was not much incentive to cheer. The next moment our sorrow was turned into joy, for a lady, (God bless her,) in a nearby house flung to the breeze a beautiful American flag, the stars and stripes fairly dancing in the sunlight. A mighty cheer arose and the 117th rushed forth and rescued a number of northern soldiers who were being transported to a southern prison. Among those rescued were a few members of the 117th, but the poor fellows had so changed in appearance that they were hardly recognized by their old comrades.

Who will say that the sight of the old flag on that day did not fill the 117th with a new courage and inspiration that characterized the regiment during the years of that remarkable conflict?

Trusting that the presentation of our old flags to the Oneida Historical Society on Tuesday may imbue a new spirit of patriotism into the hearts of the youth of Oneida County.

I am, yours very truly,

JOHN M. MARRIOTT, Vernon.
Serg. Co. E. 117th N. Y. Vols.

FROM COLONEL J. G. GRINDLAY.

The standard of a regiment is a telegraph in the center of the battle to speak the changes of the day to the wings. "Defend the flag? Rally on the colors!" is the first cry and first thought of a soldier. The standard contains the honor of the regiment, and the brave press around its bearer. The position of color bearer is one of equal honor and danger. The colors of the 146th, (three in number,) were never lost; the first and second were returned to the war department and the Governor of the State, respectively, after many battles, torn and tattered, but not dishonored, and the third given into the care and custody of the Oneida County Historical Society. They were ever gallantly borne and bravely defended by the men of the regiment, defiantly shaken in the very jaws of death, and often triumphantly waved by them on fields of victory. They were borne in the following engagements: Fredericksburg, Chancellorsville, Gettysburg, Williamsport, Bristoe Station, Rappahannock Station, Mine's Run, Wilderness, Spottsylvania, Piricy Branch Church, Laurel Hill, Bayle's House, North Anna, Tolopotomy, Cold Harbor, Bethesda Church, White Oak Swamp, Petersburg, Weldon Railroad, Poplar Spring Church, Hatcher's Run, (first and second,) Hicksford Raid, White Oak raid, Five Forks, Appomattox Court House.

JAMES G. GRINDLAY, Albany.
Col. 146th N. Y. Vols.

FROM CAPTAIN C. P. MAHAN.

I went out with the 146th Regiment and remained in the field until the close of the war. I was with the regiment almost continually, except for three or four months at division headquarters doing guard duty. I was one of the number that returned to Utica at the close of the war, and we had a grand reception. We gave the people a drill. I believe there was only eighty-one of us at that time. Our commanding officer wrote the name of each battle on our discharges. My company was Company G, the color company. I have not said much about the old flags, but I can talk it over with the boys better than I can write. My company was in the following battles: Fredericksburg, Chancellorsville, Gettysburg, Williamsport, Manassas Gap, Rappahannock Station, Bristow Station, Mine's Run, Wilderness, Laurel Hill, Spottsylvania, North Anna, Tolopotomy, Bethesda Church, Petersburg, Weldon Railroad, Chappel House, and about fifty skirmishes.

C. P. MAHAN, Clinton.
Corp. Co. G, 146th N. Y. Vols.

FROM C. M. SOMERS, ASS'T SURGEON.

There is no lack of old time inspiration, but I am paralyzed and helpless, and unable to collect my thoughts in an orderly way.

I send my abiding love to the colors of the grand 146th N. Y., and consign my lasting interest to the keeping of the Oneida Historical Society.

C. M. SOMERS, M. D., Deansboro.
Assistant Surgeon, 146th N. Y. Vol.

From Lieutenant A. P. Case.

The 146th N. Y. was taken by Colonel Garrard of U. S. Army, to the 3d Brigade, 2d Division, 5th Corps, General Sykes, the other brigades being regulars. General Weed commanding the brigade was killed at Gettysburg, and succeeded by Colonel Garrard. Colonel Jenkins, who took the regiment, was killed at Wilderness, and succeeded by Colonel Grindlay. The 146th had in all 1,568 men; 7 officers and 162 men killed in battle, 525 wounded, 550 discharged for wounds and disabilities, 327 mustered out. It was three times complimented in general orders for distinguished gallantry. Its monument on little round top, Gettysburg, stands by the side of General Warren's bronze statue, and with the sanction of New York State Gettysburg comrades bears the inscription. "From this point Major General Meade commanded the battle of July 3d."

The flag tells its own story, and that of the brave men who carried it, by the list of twenty-two battles on its folds, as authorized by the war department.

To the soldier in the field his flag means far more than it does to the peaceful citizen, who only sees it idly floating above public buildings, or as drapery at a festival. To him it stands for the strength and honor of his country, and the more it is torn by shells and bullet, the dearer it becomes.

A. P. Case, Vernon.
1st Lieut. and Q. M., 146th N. Y. Vols.

From A. H. Palmer.

I deem it an honor, of which I am proud, to have a voice in the formal turning over of the distinguished banners of the dear old 146th Regiment. Belonging to Co. C, I was almost constantly under its folds for three years. It was the color company. I was for a time one of the color guard and was proud of the association with "old glory," an object so inspiriting and ennobling.

But more than all else is it rendered sacred to me when I think of the precious lives lost in defending it on many bloody battlefields. More conspicuous than others and deeply impressed on my heart, are the gallant officers, Jenkins, Curran and Freeleigh. Braver and truer men never led men to battle in any country.

Many of our boys deserve more than a passing notice. I hope our boys living will do them justice, and I can not refrain from mentioning Private Henry Wood, son of James Wood of South street. Henry and I enlisted at the same time, and he was my tentmate. The last time I saw him to recognize him was in the line of battle, which was just advancing on the enemy at Hatcher's Run, I think it was in the winter of 1864. I was at the time mounted orderly on Gen. Fred Winthrop's staff, and as we struck the enemy's line of battle the line of battle opened at the right of my old regiment to let the General and staff ride through. In passing I caught Henry's eye. He raised his musket, pointing it to the front, intimating to me that he would give them his best. A moment later and the clash came. My dear tentmate was cut down with many others. On came the enemy with crushing force. Our lines gave way and were rallied again and again. But we were forced back a distance of about five miles, contesting the right of every foot. At last reinforcements came and we then retraced our footsteps, sweeping the enemy before us, until we regained all the ground lost, and the possession of our dead and wounded. Among them was my dear old tentmate. As we advanced he was waving his sash and cheering for victory, although exhausted from the loss of blood, and from which he never recovered.

The writer of this was present at the presentation of the banner to the 146th Regiment, if I remember right by the ladies of Oneida County. I was with this banner in camp, on the march and on the battlefield, and was one of the fragment of the regiment to return home with the colors. And, oh, what joy was ours as the colors flaunted proudly through the streets of Utica, escorted by our old and anxious friends on that beautiful July morning in 1865, to know that they had been unfurled to the breeze of many a battlefield, and never disgraced.

With pride and pleasure I voice my willingness to commit the keeping of the sacred treasure to the Oneida Historical Society. Regretting my inability to be present on the 14th, and thanking you for your generous interest in my old regiment, I am, with great respect,

Yours truly,

A. H. PALMER, Omaha, Neb.

Company C, 146th N. Y. Vols.

FROM COLOR SERGEANT ROGERS.

During the service of over four years the flags of the 2d'N. Y. H. A. were carried through eighteen battles and never fell into the hands of the enemy. At the battle of Deep Bottom, Va., when all of the color guards and the two color sergeants were either killed or wounded, a young boy by the name of Billy Wilson sprang forward and grasping one of the flags, carried it through every battle and skirmish up to the time of the muster out of the regiment without receiving an injury. Our total loss on the color guard I am unable to state, but we lost seven sergeants while carrying the colors.

HARVEY ROGERS, Seneca Falls.

Color Sergeant, 1st Lieut. Co. K, 2d N. Y. H. A.

FROM JOSEPH PORTER.

The history of the old flags of the Second N. Y. H. A. is the real history of the regiment from 1861 to 1865. A grand, reliable regiment in Hancock's Second Corps, Barlow's First Division. Enlisting under the call for the first 300,000 men, as light artillery, the regiment was mustered into the United

States service on Staten Island in the fall of 1861. From there it was sent to the fortifications on the south side of the Potomac and remained there until August 25, 1862, when it was sent with the first Mass. H. A. to join Pope at Warrenton, Va., and encountered the advance of Stonewall Jackson at Bull Run on the 27th. Here these two regiments kept at bay the 27,000 troops under Jackson from early dawn to 3 P. M. This was the result of missapprehension on the part of the enemy, who supposed we were the vanguard of Fitz John Porter's Corps from the Peninsula. The regiment lost 150 in prisoners, and was at once relegated to the defense of Washington opposite Georgetown, where it remained until the middle of May, 1864, when it was ordered to join Grant at the Wilderness, and the career of the regiment from Spottsylvania to Appomattox was one of which every member may well be proud. It was in fifteen general engagements and never lost any of its colors. The Second N. Y. H. A. was a truly cosmopolitan regiment, embodying men from every part of the State, of every nationality and walk in life. It numbered from first to last 5,000 men, of whom 500 died in the service. About one-half of the companies were from Central New York. Company E, the color company, was largely from Otsego and Oneida Counties, and commanded by Captains George Klinck and D. C. Stoddard of Utica. The regiment had two colonels from Oneida County, Colonel Jeremiah Palmer, formerly of Oriskany, and Colonel O. G. Hulser of Forestport. So it is most fitting and appropriate that the old flags of the Second N. Y. H. A. be presented to the Oneida County Historical Society for future preservation.

Co. E, Second N. Y. H. A.

JOSEPH PORTER, Rome.

FROM SERGEANT J. F. WHITING.

The Second New York Heavy Artillery was mustered into the United States service on Staten Island, October 15, 1861, and while there Governor Morgan's wife presented the regiment with a flag. Soon after we were sent to Washington and occupied forts near Alexandria, Va. The first time our flags were in service was at the battle of Second Bull Run, August 27, 1862. I volunteered February 17, 1864, and was assigned to Co. C, and from that date was with the regiment and the flag until the close of the war.

The dear old flag was carried into the following battles: Bull Run, August 27, 1862; Spottsylvania, May 12 to 19, 1864; North Anna Run, May 22, 1864; Tolopotomy Creek, May 31, 1864; Cold Harbor, June 3 to 10, 1864; Petersburg, June 16 to 22, 1864; Strawberry Plain July 28, 1864; Deep Bottom, August 14 to 16, 1864; Reams Station, August 28, 1864; Hatcher's Run, December 9, 1864; Patrick Station, March 25, 1865; Five Forks, March 31, 1865; South Side Railroad, April 2, 1865; Amelia Springs, April 6, 1865; Farmville, April 7, 1865; surrender of Lee, April 9, 1865. Twenty or more times our flags were carried into battle. Their tattered and bullet riddled condition amply proves that they were carried by true and loyal men. When one was shot down another took them up and proudly carried them to victory.

They were the last flags to leave the scene of Lee's surrender at Appomatox. Our regiment was ordered to convey the artillery and munitions of war to a place of safety, and if I mistake not they were the last flags to leave Washington for home.

JAMES F. WHITING, Middleville, N. Y.
First Sergeant, Co. C, 2d N. Y. H. A.

FROM SERGEANT WILLIAMSON.

In 1862 I had the honor of being color sergeant of the regiment. The names of the battles inscribed on one banner, by authority of the war department, illustrates the valor and loyalty of the old Second Artillery much better than anything I can say: Bull Run, Spottsylvania, North Anna, Tolopotomy, Cold Harbor, Petersburg, Strawberry Plain, Deep Bottom, Reams Station, Hatchers Run, Patrick Station, Five Forks, Southside Railroad, Amelia Springs, Farmville, Surrender of Lee.

The Second Artillery was one of seven regiments comprising the First Brigade. First Division, Second Army Corps, commanded by such glorious chiefs as W. S. Hancock, Francis C. Barlow, A. A. Humphrey and N. A. Miles. The regiment was several times complimented by special orders for its gallantry and firmness in action The colors of the old Second Artillery were never disgraced by any cowardly action on the part of their defenders, nor were they even in the possession of a traitor.

I am glad the dear old flags are now to be placed in the safe and honorable keeping of the Oneida Historical Society.

JOHN J. WILLIAMSON, Utica, N. Y.
Brev. Capt. Co. B, Second H. A.

FROM SERGEANT THOMAS T. EVANS.

It is many years since we marched under the flags. Many brave boys lost their lives carrying them while in action. Our Colonel, O. F. Hulser, took charge of them for some time after we were mustered out of the service, and had them in his office at the old Clinton House, Bleecker Street. It was from here, through Captain Stoddard, Utica, that the flags were placed in care of Bacon Post, and at one of our annual reunions held some years ago J. S. Aitkens was appointed custodian of them. One year ago at our reunion, held at Rome, it was unanimously voted that the flags should be placed in charge of the Oneida Historical Society, and at our last reunion, held in Utica, in October last, a like motion was made and carried unanimously. We went to the Historical Building in a body to see the old flags, and every one spoke approvingly of the action taken.

THOMAS T. EVANS, Utica.
1st Serg. Co. D, Second N. Y. H. A.

[From *Utica Daily Press*, Dec. 15, 1897.]

VETERANS AT LUNCH.

Mr. and Mrs. Thomas R. Proctor entertained a number of veterans at lunch at their home, 312 Genesee Street, at 1.30 P. M. yesterday. The reception was given in honor of Department Commander Shaw and Gen. Curtis. As the guests arrived they were introduced to Mr. and Mrs. Proctor, Col. Shaw and Gen. Curtis by Col. C. H. Ballou. Those present were G. W. Jones, Rome; E. F. Downer, Fritz Kohler, Utica; Rev. J. D. Ferguson, Perry B. Miller, Camden; J. W. Aldridge, George A. Reynolds, Utica; W. Stuart Walcott, New York Mills; A. G. Stein, Frank Miller, J. Harry Kent, Frederick Reinhardt, Dr. M. Cook, Utica; E. A. Wheeler, Waterville; George R. Farley, Prospect; Col. F. X. Meyer, Capt. Thelwin Jones, Utica; Hon. Joseph Porter, W. J. Cramond, Rome; Isaac P. Bielby, Yorkville; W. L. Ames, Col. George T. Hollingworth, A. Ecker, Henry Barnard, Utica; F. D. Leete, Oneida; Charles M. Dagwell, Charles F. Cleveland, Hon. John Kohler, John S. Aitken, Utica; James M. Smith, Timothy Dasey, Little Falls; W. A. Witherbee, Rome; Henry N. Marchisi, E. H. Risley, W. J. Supple, John H. Jones, John B. Jones, Gen. Rufus Daggett, Hon. John Buckley, Hon. Thomas Wheeler, Utica; Maj. D. B. Magill, New York Mills; James C. Bronson, Clinton; A. B. Snow, Leander W. Fiske, Boonville; B. F. Hinckley, Camden: Maj. James Miller, E. M. Clarke, David Jones, Lewis A. Jones, John H. Bailey, Jacob P. Yakey, Utica; Thomas Byrnes, Rome; Alfred Sears, John O'Brien, Wesley

Dimbleby, Jacob Irion, Louis Wanner, C. H. Searle, D. C. Hurd, Utica; Alonzo King, Oriskany; Clinton Beckwith, Herkimer; A. J. Budlong, Frankfort; Enoch Jones, Rouse B. Maxfield, H. I. Johnson, E. A. Tallman, George S. Dana, Joseph Wicks, H. S. Hastings, Richard Richards, J. A. Omans, H. Y. Purcell, D. C. Stoddard, Edward Lee, T. W. Wright, H. H. Timmerman.

The lunch was an elaborate one and was greatly enjoyed by the veterans. After lunch Col. Shaw moved that a vote of thanks be tendered Mr. and Mrs. Proctor for their generous hospitality. The motion was seconded by Gen. Curtis. Col. Shaw made a few complimentary remarks to the host and hostess, to which Mr. Proctor responded. The guests smoked and chatted until nearly three o'clock, when carriages were taken for the Munson-Williams Memorial. Those who had been guests at the luncheon could be easily recognized among the assemblage at the flag presentation, for each one had a small drum made of card board tied in his button hole. The ice cream was served in the drums, which were kept as souvenirs of the very pleasant feature of a memorable occasion.

The ladies who assisted with Mrs. Proctor were Mrs. W. Stuart Walcott, Mrs. A. M. Collier, Mrs. Cornelia Bacon Crittenden, Mrs. James Scott Brown, Mrs. James S. Sherman, Mrs. G. Alder Blumer, Miss A. D. Proctor, Miss L. R. Proctor, Miss Gridley, Miss Sarah B. Thomas.

At the lunch very many good things were said, and it was nearly 3 o'clock before the veterans took carriages for the Memorial.

[From *Utica Morning Herald*, Dec. 15, 1897.]

PRESENTATION OF THE FLAGS,

The battle flags of the Oneida County Regiments in the late civil war were presented to the Oneida Historical Society yesterday afternoon at the Munson-Williams Memorial, with appropriate ceremonies and eloquent addresses. Although the day was stormy and rainy there was a large attendance of veterans from all parts of the county, and every post in the county was represented. Some of the ladies who presented the flags originally were also present, as were many members of the Historical Society. The large hall was crowded to overflowing and all standing room was occupied. Two large American flags were displayed over the the front entrance, and at the left was the large picture of Fort Stanwix painted by artist Hugunine of Rome.

As they stepped upon the stage, Vice President T. R. Proctor, Gen. N. M. Curtis and Col. A. D. Shaw were heartily applauded.

The exercises began by the singing of the "Star Spangled Banner," by Elliott Stewart, the large company joining in the chorus as also did the other members of the quartette, N. H. West, A. W. Jones and G. W. Miller.

Vice President Proctor, who is also a Grand Army comrade, presided very acceptably.

Capt. A. B. Snow gave the various bugle calls, and was heartily applauded.

The 14th Regiment.

The presentation of the battle flags then took place. First in order was the Fourteenth Regiment, Col. McQuade's which was represented by Capt. James Miller, Lewis A. Jones and Color Bearers John O'Brien and Wesley Dimbleby. The flags were received by Department Commander Shaw. In presenting the flags, L. A. Jones, Secretary of the 14th Regiment Veteran Association, said:

President Proctor of the Oneida Historical Society: In behalf of the Fourteenth Regiment, New York State Volunteer Veteran Association, I place in your charge, for safe keeping, these two flags, the property of the Association.

The first is one of the United States flags of the Fourteenth New York Infantry, and it was presented to the regiment by the ladies of Utica, May 24, 1861, at Albany.

The other is the New York State banner presented by Sons of Oneida residing in New York and Brooklyn to the Oneida Volunteers, Fourteenth Regiment, N. Y. S. V., on Washington Parade Ground in New York, June 19, 1861; the presentation speech being made by Hon. Charles Tracy, a former Utican.

The remaining flag of the regiment was deposited in the State Capitol at Albany, on the return of the Fourteenth from the war, and bears this inscription:

"Colors of the Fourteenth Regiment, N. Y. S. V.; National flag, bunting; much worn; staff gone. Presented to the regiment on its departure for the field by Gov. Morgan on behalf of the State of New York, and returned to Gov. Seymour, soiled and tattered, but not dishonored." Then followed the statement "that the regiment was organized in Utica, Rome, Boonville, Batavia, Lowville, Syracuse and Hudson," with the date when it joined the Army of the Potomac, June 20

1861, and the names of the battles in which it was engaged, closing with these words: "It has the proud record that it never had its pickets driven in and never turned its back to the enemy in battle."

This inscription applies with equal force to the two flags here to-day. These colors were carried in every engagement in which the Fourteenth Regiment participated, beginning with the thirty days' siege of Yorktown, closely followed by the battles of New Bridge and Hanover Court House and one month later by that continuous engagement called the Seven Days' Battle commencing at Mechanicsville, June 26, and followed day by day by Gaines Mills, Savage Station, White Oak Swamp and closing with the great victory at Malvern Hill. In this seven days' battle out of less than 600 engaged the regiment lost fifty-four men killed and over two hundred wounded in defense of these flags and of all that these flags represented.

On the return from the Peninsula they were carried to the vicinity of Thoroughfare Gap in the second Bull Run campaign and back to the old camping ground at Miner's Hill, from thence through Washington, over South Mountain and the Antietam battle field to Shepardstown and Charlestown, W. Va., where the regiment had an engagement with Lee's rear guard. Following Lee in his retreat from Maryland the colors were carried through Harper's Ferry, up the Shenandoah Valley and through the Blue Ridge to Warrenton and from thence to Falmouth, opposite Fredericksburg. On December 13, 1862, these flags were carried in desperate charges against the rebel position behind the stone wall on Marye's Heights, in the battle of Fredericksburg, with a loss to the regiment of six killed and over 100 wounded. In May, 1863, only a few days before the expiration of its term of service, the regiment carried these colors for the last time against the enemy in the three days' battle of Chancellorsville, losing one hundred in wounded.

Returning to New York State the regiment was mustered out

of service May 24, 1863, and the flags were placed in the armory of the Utica Citizens' Corps, where they remained until the incorporation of the Fourteenth Regiment Veteran Association, since which time they have been in the care of Wesley Dimbleby, one of the trustees of the Association. When the survivors of the Fourteenth Regiment gaze upon these battle smoked and bullet torn colors scenes of the Virginia fighting days come back to us. Memories of camp life, of long and wearisome marches, of army songs and army singers, of army drill and army discipline, of picket guard, of siege and skirmish and battle, of the wounded and dying, of the dear comrades sleeping their last sleep in Virginia.

To every surviving member of the Fourteenth Regiment these flags are the most precious relics of the war. In defence of these colors the members of the regiment knew by personal experience the meaning of hard fighting, of privation, of constant association with danger and death.

Notwithstanding that our old flags are so precious to us we respond willingly and with grateful hearts to the kind invitation of the Oneida Historical Society to place our colors in this beautiful building in the case so graciously provided by you, Mr. President, and thank you for the privilege of visiting this place on each recurring 17th day of May, to salute our dear old flags. We hope that they will remain here for many, many years, an object lesson in patriotism.

The 26th Regiment.

The flags of the Twenty-Sixth Regiment were carried by Charles F. Cleveland and Joseph Keene. In presenting them Maj. Ezra F. Wetmore said:

Mr. President and Members of the Historical Society: It is a commendable desire to obtain data for history. As I was but a unit of the 26th Regiment organization, I am unable to give names of persons who were donors. This flag was presented to the regiment by Judge Smith of Oneida County, on behalf of the ladies of Utica, on the 27th day of May, 1861, at Elmira. This flag was carried on all the marches and through the battles in which the regiment was engaged which are the following: Cedar Mountain, August 6, 1862; Rappahannock Station, August 20, 21, 22; Thoroughfare Gap, August 27; Groveton or Second Bull Run, August 30; Chantilly, September 1; South Mountain, September 14; Antietam, September 17: Fredericksburg, December 13. Chancellorsville, May 23, 24, 1863. In the several battles 342 men fell beneath its folds. Three men received medals of honor for gallantry and meritorious services, viz.: Thomas Keene, Martin Shriber and Charles Cleveland. After the regiment was disbanded this flag was taken care of by Judge Bacon for several years. He placed it in charge of Post Bacon, in whose care it has remained until the present time. We cheerfully surrender this treasured relic to your care, knowing you have the proper receptacle to preserve it; and may the same spirit which prompted the members of the regiment to deeds of patriotism and daring, inspire every citizen of the United States until time shall cease to be.

Major Wetmore commanded the 26th Regiment at South Mountain, Antietam, Fredericksburg and Chancellorsville.

The 97th Regiment

Capt. Archibald B. Snow of the 97th Regiment, said—

Mr. President, Officers and Members of the Oneida Historical Society: On behalf of the Veteran Association of the 97th Regiment, I regret to say that we are compelled to appear before you empty handed to-day. Our flags are in the capitol building at Albany. We petitioned the Governor, and almost up to the last moment hoped to present them to your honorable society on this memorable occasion; but we are informed that once deposited at Albany they are looked upon as State property, and can not be secured except by legislation. Legislation will be invoked and no effort will be spared to secure our colors, to the end that they may be deposited here in this building, than which they can have no fitter final resting place. The State flag known as the Conkling flag, a blue silk field upon which the State arms were embroidered by the patriotic hands of Mrs. Roscoe Conkling, presented to Col. Charles Wheelock by the great senator himself, and the stars and stripes, our battle flag, presented to the regiment in 1861 at its place of rendezvous, by the patriotic ladies of the village of Boonville, can no more properly be considered State property, than the historic sword presented to Col. Wheelock by the ladies of Boonville, and now the most treasured heirloom in possession of his family.

To this city, the home and final resting place of the great senator and, without doubt, that also of his honored wife and widow, should the Conkling flag be brought and to this city should come also the battle flag of the Third Oneida, unfurled upon thirty battle fields, riddled and shot torn, under whose folds, with weapons in their hands and with faces to the foe, one hundred and eighty-one officers and men, died in their tracks. Here, at the central point in the territory, from which their fathers rallied in the time of their country's needs, future generations should have safely deposited and in sight those treasured relics as object lessons from age to age, teaching patriotism, and reminding them of what their fathers did and who their fathers were.

I said we came empty handed, but not entirely so. Since I arrived in this city I have the honor to meet the president of the organization by which our flag was made, Mrs. L. C. Childs, who, I am happy to say, is with us to-day. I present a history of the 97th regiment, in which is a picture of the battle flag of the regiment, on which are inscribed the names of 30 battles in which we participated. This will be kept in the case until we can substitute for it the flag itself. I have also another copy of the book for your library.

The 117th Regiment

The members of the 117th were asked to rise and as they did so, Gen Curtis also arose and said: "I believe I am an honorary member." [Applause.] Gen. Rufus Daggett presented the flag, saying:

Mr. President and Comrade: In 1862 this flag was prepared by the ladies of Utica and sent to the 117th New York Volunteers (then at the front), with the following letter and charge:

"To the Officers and men of the 117th New York Volunteers:

"The ladies of Utica, desirous of evincing their interest in the great work you have undertaken and their faith in you, the sons of Oneida, have prepared this banner with its motto chosen from your national anthem, which they hope will be satisfactory to you all, reminding you at once of the high responsibility which we devolve upon you, the chosen defenders of our liberty and happiness of the dear ones you have left behind, whose honor is inseparably bound up with your own, and above all, of your duty towards and your dependence on that higher power without whose aiding hand non ' can prosper.

"This is no time for words and we have but few to give you. Go forward with a will, bearing bravely on the glorious banner which is the ensign of all we hold most dear. Come back when your work is done, and well done, bringing this same emblem, torn and defaced it may be, but bearing only honorable marks which shall add a glow of thankfulness and pride to the heart of every maiden, wife and mother whose hopes rest so fondly upon each of you; or, come not back to us again forever. Sorrow we can bear; disgrace, never. But this is a word which, in connection with you of the One Hundred and Seventeenth, we need not use. Oneida has not known its meaning and we feel assured that it is not at your hands she will be taught it.

"Take therefore, our banner and with it receive our prayers for your safety, your happiness, your glory and above all, for the safety of the land which you go forth to defend and redeem. In behalf of the ladies,

"Respectfully yours,
"(Signed.)   L. C. GRAHAM.
"Utica, October, 1862.

How faithfully and well these injunctions were carried out by the regiment, the list of engagments, the killed, the wounded and missing in battle, the deaths from disease during its three years of service, will tell you, and surely proves it was true to to the trust, and after thirty-two years the survivors of the regiment bring it to you, tattered, torn and bullet-riven, with a list of the engagements in which it was carried.

Hoping that as its history shall be read and better known, it may inspire in the young men and women a greater love for their country and flag. Mr. President we now surrender to you for safer keeping this dear old flag. [Applause.]

The following is a list of the engagements in which the 117th Regiment New York State Volunteers participated: Siege of Suffolk, Va., 1863; Hanover Junction, Va., July, 1863; Siege of Fort Wagner, 1863 and 1864; Swift's Creek, Va., 1864; Drury's Bluff, Va., May, 1864; Cold Harbor, Va., June, 1864; Petersburg Heights, Va., June 15, 1864; Siege of Petersburg, seventy-one days in the trenches; Cemetery Hill, Va., July 30, 1864; Chapin's Farm, Va., September 29, 1864; Darbytown Road, Va., October 27, 1864; Fort Fisher, N. C., January 15, 1865; Fort Anderson, N. C., 1865.

Comrade G. B. Fairhead read the following verses written by by him in honor of the 117th Regiment, entitled "The Old Banner of the Fourth Oneida."

Ye tattered shreds of faded silk,
    Patches worn dim in war's wild fray,
All marred and torn by shot and shell,
    Say! Are ye worth a thought to-day?

A thought? Ah, yes! And floods of tears;
    Then a rare shout both loud and long,
Inwove with patriots' truest troth,
    For every shred deserves a song.

When first your beauty met the view
    Of Fouth Oneida's stalwart boys,
Drawn up in compact, hollow square,
    'Twas then ye quickened hero vows.

Love's benisons ye bore to us
    From women of this city fair,
Whose loyal hearts beat quick and warm,
    Entreating us to do and dare.

They said "Our prayers will follow this
    That it be borne with high endeavor,
Then homeward come, if with 'well done,'
    'Or come not back forever.'"

Then with our triple flags we faced
    The brave man's march, the toil, the fight;
The Color Guard, valiant and true,
    The centre of our hero might.

When war clouds broke so hot and fierce,
    Those banners met with rent and gash;
There noble men beneath them fell,
    And many felt the battle's crash.

Nor faltered they, till victory came,
    No loss of star, no spot on stripe,
But doubly dear for val'rous men,
    Were yielded for the Nation's life.

Dear Tatters, wet with tears and blood,
    We yield you to the city's care,
Demanding they devoutly keep
    What cost our ranks such value rare.

                      GEORGE B. FAIRHEAD.

Co. D, 117th N. Y. Vols.

The 146th Regiment

The flag of the 146th Regiment was presented by William Campbell, who said:

In behalf of the 146th Regiment, New York State Volunteers, whose cause I have the honor to represent, I surrender to your care and keeping this old regimental flag. You will find it sadly tattered and worn, a mere remnant of its former self. Like ourselves, it is chiefly valuable, not for what it is, but for it represents. We commenced following it before the battle of Fredericksburg, December 13, 1862, and we did not cease to follow it until after Appomattox 1865. We commenced to follow it when young, strong and brave, for we were one of the 300 fighting regiments, with something like 1,000 men. Whether we followed it to victory or defeat we never allowed it to trail in the dust or know a surrender. It was and is a symbol to our devotion to the cause of freedom and humanity. We surrender it to you to-day because we, like it, are only a remnant, and while we are passing beyond the ability to care for it or protect it, it will remain as a reminder of our sacrifice and loyalty. Cherish it heartily. Care for it tenderly, that it may remain among you to remind the young of coming generations of deeds done and accomplished by the old Garrard Tigers.

Concerning this flag Gen. James G. Grindley writes: "The standard of a regiment is a telegraph in the center of the battle to speak the changes of the day to the winds. 'Defend the flag! rally on the colors!' is the first cry and first thought of a soldier. The standard contains the honor of the regiment, and the brave press around its bearer. The position of color bearer is one of equal honor and danger. The colors of the 146th (three in number) were never lost; the first and second were returned to the War Department and the Governor of the State, respectively, after many battles, torn and tattered, but not dishonored, and the third given into the care and custody of the Oneida Historical Society. They were gallantly borne and bravely defended by the men of the regiment, defiantly shaken in the very jaws of death, and often triumphantly waved by them on fields of victory. They were borne in the following engagements: Fredericksburg, Chancellorsville, Gettysburg, Williamsport, Bristoe Station, Rappahannock Station, Mine Run, Wilderness, Spottsylvania, Piriey Branch Church, Laurel Hill, Gayle's House, North Anna, Tolopotomy, Cold Harbor, Bethesda Church, White Oak Swamp. Petersburg, Weldon Railroad, Poplar Spring Church, Hatcher's Run, (first and second,) Hicksford Raid, White Oak Raid, Five Forks, Appomattox Court House."

The following order, copied from the official order book of the regiment, speaks for itself, and you may deem it worthy of incorporating in your account of the exercises on the 14th inst.

(Order No. 15.)
Headquarters 146th N. Y. Vols.,
Near Three Mile Station, Va.,
November 1, 1863.

The regiment has just received with proper solemnities a new stand of colors, and it has now to transmit to the Governor of the State of New York, the old flag whose tattered folds will speak more eloquently than words of the work which the sons of New York are performing in behalf of the country. It will recall the hard fought fields of Frederickburg, Chancellorsville and Gettysburg. To some it may bring a tear of remembrance for the brave dead who have fallen in its defence. It will never cause a cheek to blush with shame. Fight under the new flag as gallantly as you have done under the old, and you may hope ere another year passes to carry it back to your homes, to receive the thanks of a grateful country.

By order of Col. DAVID T. JENKINS.
WM. WRIGHT, Lieut. and Actg. Adjt., 146th N. Y. Vols.

This is the flag under which the heroic Jenkins yielded up his life for national immortality, while bravely leading his regiment in the charge at the terrible Battle of the Wilderness, and which was saved from capture that day by J. Albert Jennison.

The 2d New York Heavy Artillery

The flags of the Second New York Heavy Artillery, including guidons, were then presented. The address was made by Capt. D. C. Stoddard, who said:

Mr. President and Members of the Oneida Historical Society: The surviving comrades of the Second New York Heavy Artillery Volunteers, through its regimental organization, here offers to your honorable Society the flags of that regiment, earnestly requesting you to accept the custody and preservation of them as a perpetual trust. You, on your part, undertaking always to keep them in some suitable and public place in this beautiful building, that shall be open and accessible to them and the public at all seasonable times, to be regulated by yourselves.

They are emblematic in their meaning. The stars and stripes represent the United States and its authority over all who serve under them. The other flag by its emblem, denotes the State enrolling the regiment as volunteers, and its color and cross cannon show the branch of service in which it served.

In service they are borne and guarded by choice men from the ranks, carefully selected for this post of honor, for their well known strength, endurance and bravery, and though a post of hardship and danger to be one of the color guard is eagerly sought for and greatly prized when obtained.

In line of battle the flags are in the center of the regiment to guide and control the two wings while maneuvering and are also the rallying point in case of confusion or disaster.

Their loss from any cause in battle is considered a disgrace upon every member of the regiment, and to throw them away or abandon them in danger is not only a most disgraceful military act, but severely punished.

Every officer and enlisted man loves, honors and is proud of the colors under which he serves and never ceases to do so as long as life lasts. To see them revives many a thought and feeling of the time when they were his especial care, some may be pleasant and more sad, but yet he likes to bring them to mind, shed a tear for a fellow comrade and "fight over again the battles" of his youth. And when he is gone, that they will still remain to remind those that come after him that it is also their duty to defend to the uttermost their country in every peril to the extent of their lives and fortune, and to hand it down to their children with not a star less upon the National flag.

The Second New York Heavy Artillery Volunteers was not strictly an Oneida County Regiment, and yet we believe that more men served in it from this county and vicinity than any regiment which was organized within it and called by its name. In the summer of 1861 an artillery regiment was attempted to be organized, with its camp upon Staten Island, but it did not prosper, nor had any company the minimum number of men sufficient to be mustered as a company. While in this condition the Governor authorized Jeremiah Palmer, then living at Oriskany, who had been connected with the uniformed militia and favorably known here and in this vicinity, to fill up and organize a full artillery regiment from this nucleus of men on Staten Island.

He entered upon his task with energy and three companies were recruited from this city, one from Jefferson County and two from Frankfort, Herkimer County, and the other six companies were filled up and mustered into the service. Early in November, 1861, the regiment was in forts doing garrison duty in the "Defenses of Washington South of the Potomac."

At this time the field officers of the regiment were: Colonel; Jeremiah Palmer; Lieutenant Colonel, Henry P. Roach; Majors,

Alexander Douel and William A. McKay; Adjutant, Ezra D. Corwin; Quartermaster, George N. Mead.

The Captains of original companies were: Company A, Thomas Maguire; Company B, J. Howard Kitching; Company C, George Hogg; Company D, John D. Jones; Company E, George Klinck; Company F, James Houseman; Company G, Thomas J. Clark; Company H, Charles L. Smith; Company I, Abner C. Griffin; Company K, Plinley L. Joslin; Company L, James L. Hulser; Company M, Emiel P. Halstead.

The regiment had as Colonels besides the above Gustave Wagner, Milton Cogswell and J. V. G. Whistler, both of the Regular Army.

If possible, and time permitted, we would gladly mention every officer and enlisted man who at any time belonged to this regiment and take great pleasure in detailing the many acts of bravery which each performed, but it is impossible, as more than 4,000 names were borne upon its rolls.

With what pleasure and satisfaction we could read to you that long, fatal roll of honor of comrades who died or were killed in battle, or to give the names of those fifty brave comrades who died in rebel prisons and read the names of the "missing" who sleep peacefully in graves unknown, but alas this we cannot do. All these names are worthy to be recorded in letters of gold upon sacred tablets as those who gave their lives in maintaining equal rights and justice for their fellow-men.

In the regimental casualties in the volunteer regiments for the whole war this regiment stands in the third grade—all suffered in eleven months of service in the field.

The first experience of war came to the regiment when alone and upon the march to join Gen. Pope a few days before the second Bull Run Battle was fought, just as the regiment desired to pass through Manassas Junction. Stonewall Jackson with his corps blockaded the way and opened upon it with his artillery, as well as sending his cavalry upon our flanks and rear, which was resisted for little time, when it was believed best to get out of Jackson's way by the shortest route and quickest time, and which we did by a loss of 100 wounded and prisoners. This we always defended upon the ground that if we could not whip Jackson he would defeat us—and that "discretion was the better part of valor," and that

> "He who fights and runs away,
> May live to fight another day."

And we proved this to be true.

After this we were returned to the forts and to garrison duty. Early in 1863 Col. J. N. G. Whistler, a graduate of West Point, was made Colonel, and every company was filled to overflowing with recruits, making it 2,000 strong. The Colonel instituted the strictest discipline, maintained company and battalion drills, organized schools of instruction for officers and men, and before the spring of 1864 no better disciplined and drilled volunteer regiment was in service.

Early in May 1864, the regiment was ordered to join the Army of the Potomac as infantry with other heavy artillery regiments forming a division under the command of Gen. R. O. Tyler, and joined it at Spottsylvania. Within two or three days this division was attacked by Ewell's corps, and a sharp action ensued, lasting four or five hours, when the confederates were repulsed, the division losing 2,500 to 3,000 killed, wounded and missing; this regiment losing 250. The "Heavies" were complimented by an order from army headquarters for good conduct in their first fight.

Immediately thereafter the regiment was assigned for service to the First Brigade, Col. Nelson A. Miles commanding, (now Commander-in-Chief U. S. Army) First Division, Gen. Francis C. Barlow commanding, Second Corps, Major Gen. Winfield Scott Hancock commanding, where it did duty until its muster out of service in September, 1865.

Its history during this time is interwoven with that of the gallant Second Corps; wherever that Corps went, it went also, and in danger and battle performed its whole duty, meriting and receiving the commendation of its commanding officers and the respect of those serving immediately with them.

All along that fatal road, that continuous fighting ground of those great and brave armies, from the fatal Spottsylvania to the victorious Appomatox Court House, are the graves of its brave dead; while many times more of its brave men bear ugly scars of cruel wounds received by them in these fatal conflicts. This could not be otherwise; our foes were of the same blood, as brave and steadfast in battle as ourselves, and were only conquered after both men and means were exhausted wherewith to longer continue the struggle.

Then let us ever respect those foes, which withstood our armies so valiantly, so long and so bravely; and may this country ever keep united in national fraternity, unity and devotion to its flag.

In conclusion, we hope and trust that the services of the Second New York Heavy Artillery Volunteers in aiding to subdue those organized armies of the great rebellion, will appear to you worthy to have its colors placed in the archives of your society, where for all time they may be kept and preserved in remembrance of the brave men who in danger guarded and protected them until this day.

Third New York Light Artillery

Lieutenant C. F. King, Rome, of the Third New York Light Artillery, said the regiment did not have its flag, but it had a guidon which it would present as soon as suitable action was taken by the Regimental Association.

Gen. McQuade's Flags

In presenting the General McQuade flags and the flag made by the daughters of Hon. Alrick Hubbell, Lewis A. Jones was accompanied by Gen. McQuade's grandsons as color bearers. He said:

Mr. President: I am requested by Mrs. James Scott Brown the daughter of Gen. James McQuade, to present to the Oneida Historical Society, three flags. The first is Gen. McQuade's Headquarters Flag of the 2d Brigade, 1st Division, 5th Army Corps, and the color bearers for this occasion are two grandsons of Gen. McQuade, Masters James McQuade Brown and James McQuade. The second is the Headquarters Flag of the 5th Army Corps, and the color bearer is Samuel Lane McQuade, also a grandson of General McQuade. The third is a Palmetto Flag captured at the battle of Malvern Hill by John O'Brien and Peter Pickler of the 14th Regiment, and by them turned over to Gen McQuade who was an eye-witness of the affair. The color bearer for this flag is Charles S. Brown, 2d, a fourth grandson of the General.

Chaplain Ferguson proposed three cheers for the flags and the boys and they were given with a will.

A Confederate Flag

John B. Jones of the 115th, said: At the request of Gen. Daggett I present for him an emblem of the confederacy, a confederate signal flag, taken from the hands of a confederate at the greatest battle of the time, Fort Fisher. [Applause.] Stained with the blood of some confederates. He has requested me to present it to you, and it bears an appropriate inscription. [Applause.]

President Proctor's Response.

President Proctor then, on behalf of the Oneida Historical Society, said:

Men and Women, Comrades: With gratitude, with reverence and with a full appreciation of its responsibilities the Oneida Historical Society accepts the care and custody of these precious treasures.

This Society wishes to make public acknowledgement to the patriotic men and women who have so unselfishly placed these flags in its keeping. This gracious and generous act will enable it to extend its usefulness in a great degree.

It is with especial pleasure that the Society welcomes these noble women who, with others of blessed memory, furnished and presented some of these flags to Oneida County Regiments more than a third of a century ago.

These flags will be placed in yonder hall, where they will be beyond the touch, but in sight of all who may wish to see them; and there they will stand as monuments to McQuade and Davies, to Lowery and Bagg, to Hunt and Curran, to Bacon and Skilling, to Pease and Jenkins, to Reynolds and Bright, and to all the other brave and noble men who risked their lives to save their country—and there they will remain until they shall have crumbled into dust.

Here, year after year so long as any of them shall remain, will come these veterans and their associates to salute their colors and to revive their friendships, and they will go out from here with renewed vigor for their every day work.

And here will be established a silent school of patriotism,

THOMAS R. PROCTOR.

where those who in the natural order must succeed us, will come and point with pride to the colors under which their fathers fought, and they will be inspired to better lives, to broader and nobler citizenship and to a higher manhood.

Let us believe that in that bright citadel of peace—that far off camp beyond the skies where so many of the Grand Army have already been mustered, that to-day our comrades there are joining with us in singing praises to the God of battle, who in his infinite wisdom and mercy vouchsafed to us the final victory.

The address was a feeling and eloquent one and at its close many were moved to tears.

Major Miller proposed three cheers for Comrade Proctor, and never were cheers given more heartily.

Mr. Proctor said: I am much obliged by this unexpected expression of your esteem and confidence.

Chaplain Ferguson's Prayer.

Prayer was then offered by Chaplain J. V. Ferguson, who said:

Unto thee, oh God, the giver of all good and the source of all blessing, we come with hearts full of tenderness and of gratitude for thy wonderful mercies shown to us as a people and for the generous guidance that has made possible the exercises of this hour. We all know Thee, oh Lord, for the national blessings that have come to us. From the earliest period it was evident that the God of battles and of nations was caring for his people. Through thy great kindness and the inspiration thou hast given to the family to erect this structure so beautiful and grand that shall perpetuate its memory, adorn the city and bless the community by being the receptacle of these tokens and emblems that have been held so dear, not only to those who have shared common dangers under them, but for the services of those by whom these shattered relics came down to us with no record of dishonor or neglected duty to mar their importance. While these emblems have so large a place and so strong a hold on our affections, they tell again the story of long marches and tired feelings, and of almost impassable barriers surmounted; of burdens almost too heavy for humanity to bear. But we thank Thee that they come back with no less of determination to do their whole duty. They tell of dangers of the battlefield and of terrible missiles that struck down so many comrades. They tell of heroes who fell with the face to the foe, and so they shall ever bear the testimony we so love to hear of patriotism and devotion to heart and life and the grand work of American

Citizens. We praise Thee for the emancipation of four mllion citizens from their shackels. We thank Thee for perpetuity in all lines and everything that has given the country so advanced a position among the nations of the world and that its flag is respected and honored wherever known. We pray for a continuance of thy favor. May its rulers be men who fear God and work righteousness. We pray that the virtues of morality and patriotism may be abiding principles in the heart of every citizen. Let all the citizens be imbued by these high sentiments while life shall last. We feel a sadness for those of our comrades who have gone before, but as has been so beautifully expressed, we feel that they are with us in concern on this occasion. May these flags sleep together in peace as an emblem of the unity of the land. We pray that the time may never come that any man shall lisp a word or do a deed that shall sever State from State, or city from country, but let every such action be paralyzed by the power of God. Bless the widow and orphan whose hearts are torn by thoughts of loved ones from whom they are severed. Unto Thee, oh God, and the care of this Society we now commit these flags that mean so much and are to us so dear. Care for them and us, and unto Thee shall thanks and praise be given evermore. Amen.

Address by Commander Shaw.

In introducing Commander Shaw, President Proctor said that the position of department commander had never been more ably filled than by Col. Shaw. As no department commander can be re-elected, however, I know I voice your sentiments when I nominate him for commander of the Grand Army of the United States.

The men gave three hearty cheers for Col. Shaw, and President Proctor added, "Now see that you do your duty."

Commander Shaw said:

Mr. Chairman, Comrades, Ladies and Gentlemen:

This will be an historic occasion of ever memorable interest to all present who served in the armies of the Union in the late civil war from 1861 to 1865.

During this period one of the greatest wars of the world was waged, and willing volunteers furnished the girth and grain of the heroic forces which finally wore out the brave and misguided assailants of the government of the United States. Measured in years, the stupendous conflict was short, but judged by results, it was unrivaled in the past history of nations for its importance and commanding influence in settling forever the abhorrent tyranny of slavery on our soil, and thus laying anew on unquestioned foundations of freedom and righteousness, the redeemed fabric of a free people's government in this new world.

We meet this day, comrades and citizens, to commemorate the

COL. A. D. SHAW,
Commander Department of New York G. A. R.

achievements of the volunteer soldiers who went to the war as
defenders of the Union in the period of which I have spoken;
and we are to take part in the deeply interesting exercises
connected with receiving some of the battle flags of the
Republic for safe-keeping among the rich historic treasures of
this Historical Society's fine memorial building.

A great majority of the battle flags carried by troops raised
in our great State, in the late war, are deposited at the Capitol
at Albany, and constitute touching object lessons of the
bravery and sacrifices of our volunteers. I believe, however,
that the easier it is made for the descendants of soldiers who
fought under regimental flags to visit and gaze upon them, the
richer will be the quickening fruits of the spirit of appreciation
of duties well done amid the fire and the havoc of bloody battle
fields. And so I bid you welcome to this unique and thrilling
scene—one that will never be repeated in the lives of any one
here present.

The beautiful flag of our country was born amid the throes of
the opening agonies of the new birth of freedom on this
continent. Its history is full of interest to every American.
On the sea it floated first in action over the renowned naval
hero, Paul Jones, and on the land at Fort Stanwix, it received
its first baptism of blood! Rich inheritance, this, for an ever-
lasting monument of the heroism of the defenders of this
valley, when the opening chapters of an immortal history were
being written in the blood of its brave defenders. It is the
famous emblem of our Republic, the

> " Flag of the free heart's hope and home
> By angel hands to valor given."

And it well becomes every son and daughter of our free soil
to cherish it with a love and loyalty as precious and deathless as
liberty itself.

It is not my purpose to take time in this connection to enlarge upon the glory of our flag, or in any detail review its interesting history. I shall endeavor to consider some phases of the lessons which are germane to this beautiful occasion, and which should make a deep impression upon all our minds.

The flag of a nation, from the earliest times, has represented its organized offensive and defensive power. The banners of an army have always been the idol of the rank and file. Men have again and again snatched the standard from dead or dying comrades, in the horrid havoc of battle, with a heroism as unselfish as ever illuminated the pages of history. And why? Because the flag borne high aloft in action represents the cause for which men are perilling their lives, and is, in their eyes, the sign of all that is dear to them as soldiers and patriots. In a word, it is sentiment that makes heroes, on and off the battle fields of this world. It was sentiment—that of lofty patriotism—which inspired Franklin to declare that "Where Liberty is, there is my Country," during the trying events of the Revolution. The sentiment of patriotism is the inspiration out of which heroes are made. As a rule, the environments of youth become the real characteristics of age.

New England ideas took deep root in the hearts of the rugged and stalwart early settlers of this beautiful and historic valley of the Mohawk. Upon the early battle grounds around this region were sown the seeds of heroic sacrifices in the morning dawn of the Republic; and the blood of the dauntless Herkimer and his soldiers enriched this dear soil as that of lofty-minded patriots and true heroes. The lessons taught by their bravery and death sunk deep into the hearts of the dwellers along this lovely valley, whose charming river is "Fairer than Avon and sweeter than Ayr;" and duty's stern voice has never been unheeded from the day of their death until the present hour by the loyal descendants of the soldiers of whom I have spoken.

The spirit of 1861 was a revival of the patriotic sentiments of 1776. The valor of the formative age of Washington in the development of a free government was equaled by the protective era of Lincoln, and both were fed by the same patriotic fires. Both were equal to the needs of their day and generation.

The American Revolution founded a new civilization in the wilderness of this western world over which the "Stars and Stripes" floated as the sign of its sovereignty.

In 1861 rebellion, wild and savage, struck at the nation's life with more than Titanic power, and raised a new flag, the "Stars and bars," as the hateful rival of our Revolutionary emblem. Compromises were as dust and ashes when the cry echoed over the loyal north—"They have fired upon the 'Stars and Stripes' floating over Sumter's walls." The crisis, long foreshadowed, had come at last. Reason had been defied, and the sword was unsheathed. The lips of hostile cannon were fringed with fire as the dread shots thundered against the flag of our Union and its brave defenders. The strongholds of the nation were besieged by men who were lost to the old ties of citizenship, and who were resolved to destroy the Union or lose all by the cruel arbitrament of war.

In this extreme crisis of the Union's fate, in this tremendous holocaust of blood and sacrifice, the volunteers from Oneida County went willingly forth in defense of the national authorities and to preserve and maintain the inalienable right of the majority to rule. No sublimer course ever moved men to peril their lives on cruel battle fields than this. And as the great conflict went on, and slavery after a time became an acknowledged and commanding factor in the problem of a redeemed nationality, the cause became doubly just and inspiring. Looking backward as only veterans can, and taking into view the four years of internecine strife in this epoch of transcendent glory in our country's history, it is hard to keep back the tears. Memory gilds this past with recollections of services rendered a common country, and of scenes and sacrifices beyond the power of words to describe.

These flags, if they could speak, could tell tales of valor and of blood, as they were borne in the hell of battle, which would melt in pity every heart before me. Why was all this bloodshed and the colossal destruction and burden of this war inevitable? Abraham Lincoln, the greatest ruler that ever graced and blest the earth, summed it all up in these words in his ever memorable Second Inaugural Address: "On the occasion corresponding to this, four years ago, all thoughts were anxiously directed to an impending civil war. All dreaded it; all sought to avert it. While the Inaugural Address was being delivered from this place, devoted altogether to *saving* the Union without war, insurgent agents were in the city, seeking to *destroy* it without war, seeking to dissolve the Union and divide its effects, by negotiation. Both parties deprecated war; but one of them would make war rather than let the nation survive, and the other would *accept* war rather than let it perish, and the war came." These words sound like the sayings of the prophets of old, and present the fact that an "irrepressible conflict" had come in the life of the nation. Sectionalism had divided the allegiance of the south, and led to the rebellion against the authority of the Union.

In this light, thirty-two years after the close of this unhappy and destructive Civil War, the questions arise of how best to inspire our whole people with the safe sentiments of patriotism, in the love of the flag, one country and a common nationality? I answer first, by

The Common Culture of Patriotic Teachings

In every school in the nation. It is now universally acknowledged that without sectional teachings the war of the great rebellion would have been impossible. It is the law of ages that a divided house is always in trouble. Common textbooks in all of the common schools of the Union, based upon broad principles of American history, uncolored by prejudice and just in their worthy treatment of a happily ended conflict, are the sure agencies of future concord and lasting union. Unite with these patriotic exercises, properly arranged so as to teach loyalty and love for the flag, and such drill movements as will make the body strong and beautiful, while developing the mind in patriotism and the highest citizenship, and the safety and glory of our great country will be forever assured.

A country of sections is always in danger of revolutions. A common heritage, based upon righteousness, begets sentiments of loyalty and patriotism of commanding security and peace. With us the chains of slavery and the hates of passionate war times have been buried in one common grave, that of the "dead past." There is no longer reason for irritating controversies over the settlement of a struggle which, under God, resulted in a new birth of freedom. What could not be reasoned out by voice and pen was fought out by sword and gun; and the blue and the gray have lived to unite in a common citizenship again, even more loyal to the Stars and Stripes than they were before the war began. What was taught and settled at the cannon's mouth and on the bloody battle plain, in this war period, could have been taught and peacefully settled in the schools and homes of the nation, if a broader and more unselfish policy of patriotic citizenship had been the loyal sentiment of our whole people.

The veterans of the war, south and north, realize as no one else can what war means and what war costs; and veterans are bravest and tenderest when brave soldiers win or lose in battle, in their after relations with each other. To have lived to see the sentiments of loyalty to the flag and Union become common over all the land after our bitter civil war, is a crown of glory to every veteran who periled his life to save the Union.

We are living in an age of high speed, and this calls for keen oversight to keep us on the safe track of development. We must see to it that patriotism becomes a commanding sentiment along all national lines, and that the sentiment of honor more and more becomes the inspiring glory of youth and age. To this end the stars and stripes should be cherished as the sign of American greatness and the object of our universal love.

What a beautiful sight it is to see our Nation's Flag floating over the school houses in a large number of States, educating the sentiment of loyalty to our institutions in this blessed era of reunited and commanding American citizenship. Why has this new custom of displaying the Stars and Stripes over the schools come into such widespreading observance? For the reason that the sentiment of patriotism has quickened the forces of love of flag and country as a result of the bloody struggle for the defense of our revolutionary heritage, and in redeeming the nation from the tyranny of slavery. Common sacrifices taught sober judgment after the battles ended. Reason and righteousness are in the advance in our present uplifting blessings of American civilization. Dangers there indeed are, and evils widespread and serious on every hand, but the American heart is broadly true to justice and liberty; and the teachings of Christ—the head of the world's true democracy—are making sure headway.

Lovers of American institutions should do all in their power to foster the best elements in the life of our people. Every safeguard of culture, based upon patriotic sentiments, should be universally provided and loyally maintained. Foreign countries little love our larger liberty, and foreigners still regard our Republic as a dangerous and uncertain experiment. We must therefore look for safe inspirations within our own country for our future development in obtaining a higher national life. The democratic idea of equality before the law and of equal political privileges for all good citizens should be universally and jealously guarded, and never betrayed.

Before the Mayflower, in the Old World, the classes ruled

the masses. Since Plymouth Rock became a stepping-stone for a juster religious and political creed, the masses have had control of American institutions, and their object lessons—despite irritating weaknesses in the past—of a peoples' government, have shaken the crowns on the heads of hereditary monarchs ever since. Had the Puritan and the Cavalier, from the first landing on our shores, been guided by the same principles of equality, the bloody period of secession would have been possibly avoided. With the same spirit of national culture in force on the banks of the James as there was on the shores of the Hudson, sectionalism would have been swallowed up in unity.

OUR NATIONAL MORAL FORCE.

In little over a hundred years our nation has become a mighty moral force in the world. The material development and educational opportunities have become the wonder of our great age. In peace and in war Americans have proved their right to rank among the highest and greatest statesmen and generals of history. In statesmanship, tested in new problems of government as never rulers before were tried, we present our Washington and our Lincoln. In generalship, we rest our claims with Grant as the greatest soldier, all in all, of the centuries. Thus we have in the world's view three Americans of universal reputation, as the product of our American development, within the cycle of our first century of national life. I know of no other similar and sufficient parallel. And in area and population we stand in the foremost rank of civilized peoples.

We have proved our American quality in the circles of national responsibilities in settling questions of vast difficulties in such a way as call forth the unstinted praise of the leading foreign statesmen of our time, and we have proved that we can govern ourselves and secure peace and progress through trusting all our people with the ballot.

Art is being grandly developed along all lines of culture, so that genius everywhere seeks our shores and commends our support. Our past has been glorious beyond the most sanguine prophecies of our early founders; and our future will be worthy of our great opportunities, if we are only true to ourselves. We should stand steadfastly for American Institutions, and cultivate more and more reverence for God and love of our whole country. There should be no place in American hearts for old world theories based upon hereditary wealth and power. Not exclusive privileges for the favored few but equal rights for all, is the true glory of our birthright.

The best model of righteous government is found in our country where the principles of liberty, fraternity and equality are living rights common to every child and resting on the manhood of the whole people. If eternal vigilance was truly the price of American liberty at the first, equally true must it be that eternal vigilance will be the price of safe and enduring American principles of self-government in coming years. We have won the right in a little more than a single century of national life to lead the world in all that uplifts individuals and promotes and secures their happiness and independence. The loyal duty is placed upon us of holding the vantage ground on liberty's high plane we have already won, and of making it impregnable through wise actions and loyal inspirations. Do even favored Americans fully realize what our boasted liberty has cost, and what it really represents? I sometimes fear not. If we did, we should be braver and more loyal in the defense of our blood-bought rights, and more alert and self-sacrificing in maintaining virtue and honor in our public and private life. A worthy appreciation of our birthright—bought at such a cost of heroic sacrifices, in the throes of the revolution and in the fiery furnace of the rebellion—burning in every American heart would shut out all aping of foreign ways and all alliances with titled branches of needy and decaying old aristocratic families, where bank accounts are the one almost always controlling element in the marriages of American heiresses by foreigners. I judge this to be true, because I have yet to hear of a single "love match" of this foreign sort, where an American girl without money has been sought out and married by titled personages in foreign lands. My own view is that within our country there are ample opportunities for American heiresses to marry Americans, and thus add to the elements of American possibilities within the land Americans have developed, and where American heiresses have to look for the source of their wealth!

I go a step further and say that the worthy son of a worthy American veteran is the highest rank of true manliness among men. If there is a nobler birthright than this I do not know where to look for it.

When our culture of American love for our dear country becomes a more consuming fire than it is now, we shall see less bending of the "pregnant hinges of the knee" to foreign fashions, foreign residence, foreign ideas and foreign manners, and more reverence for American rights, American rulers and American ideals from every condition in our homes and society.

I refer to these important truths here and now, because this meeting calls up memories sweet and sad of our earlier and later struggles for a people's government. I see before me veterans who had a proud part in the late war, and who marched and fought under these battle flags we shall to-day consign to the final custody of this worthy Historical Society. Only a comparatively few are present who followed them in the shock of battle, for the harvest of death has gathered them into their eternal home. When all these dear defenders are gone, these flags will long remain as object lessons of a glorious service, immortal in the annals of mankind. These silken banners will slowly crumble to dust, in future years, but the spirit that defended them and brought them forth is as eternal as the stars in the heavens. The Great Teacher of Gallilee laid it down as a great law of life that seed sown must die before the after-growth could be assured. It is even so in all patriotic teachings. The deeds of heroes become the seed of citizenship growing up into freeman equal to every duty, and blessed of God unto all good works and ways.

Another leading lesson Christ taught, in answer to ensnaring questions, was this: "Render into Cæsar the things that are Cæsar's, and unto God the things that are God's." In thus defining duties, political and spiritual, He laid down the fundamental principle of a pure democracy, and upon this profound and inspired truth rests all our hopes for the future. And Paul declared, "Look not every man on his own things, but every man also on the things of others."

The Retrospect and Prospect.

We stand too near the great events which have in part their representation here this day to fairly sum up the true grandeur of the service which our volunteers rendered humanity at large and our common country, when war's bloody tempests swept in fury over this land.

A few days ago I had placed in my hands a little volume entitled "Underground Railroad Sketches." I was riding by rail in a swiftly moving train, and as I read the simple narrative of how fugitive slaves were passed through free States to the goal of safety and freedom in Canada, I was deeply moved. Within the memory of many living, passengers on this historic underground railway were guarded and sent on their perilous way, as men and brethren, seeking the yearned for blessings of freedom. Let me read to you one incident. A colored man stands upon the auction block, dignified in manner, with serious countenance, and silent. "Now gentlemen and ladies," says the auctioneer, "I offer you a first class servant. He is honest and faithful, and moreover *he is a Christian;* no sham, I tell you, but a genuine, conscientious Christian man. He would die rather than commit a wrong act or betray his master. How much do you offer for a servant that you can depend upon every time.", I make no needless comment on this revolting scene, which actually took place just before the breaking out of the rebellion in 1861.

Looking backward it seems like a bad dream to recall the fact that there were 3,952,608 slaves in our country in the year of our Lord 1860, every one liable to be sold like animals, on the auction blocks, in slave pens. When I shut this little book and looked out upon the beautiful scenes as we swiftly passed through this valley of the Mohawk, the thoughts that surged through my soul brought the quick falling tears. Surely, I thought, the bloody sweat of almost numberless heroes, the enormous material losses, the thousands of battle-blots—all these were indeed not in vain, for the shackles fell from all the slaves before the final surrender.

"And henceforth there shall be no chain,
　Save underneath the sea,
　The wires shall murmur through the main,
　Sweet songs of liberty."

That great philosopher—one of the greatest our country or the world has ever produced,—Theodore Parker, in a discourse in Music Hall, Boston, in 1854, seven years before the war, closed his eloquent and profound speech in these prophetic words: "One day the north will rise in her majesty and put slavery under our feet, and then we shall extend the area of freedom. The blessing of Almighty God will come down upon the noblest people the world ever saw, who have triumphed over Theocracy, Monarchy, Aristocracy, Despotocracy, and have a Democracy—a government of all, for all and by all, * * * a State without a king, a community without a lord, and a family without a slave."

What a glorious prophecy was this; and you and I, comrades and citizens, who lived and fought, or supported the soldiers in the field, were partakers in its more glorious fulfillment. We saw the "one day" dawn which Theodore Parker predicted with unerring spiritual vision, in our young manhood's morning, and we this day thank God that our lot was cast amid such manifestations of true liberty. Your loyal deeds have been wrought into the world's great heart, and as we meet this remnant of as brave soldiers as ever drew sword or carried gun in war to witness the simple ceremonies of depositing the flags you loved and defended in the safe keeping of this historic monument, let me again congratulate you on this impressive scene. Whatever disappointments may have crossed the path of veterans since the war, one thing is beyond the reach of the changes and worries of this world, and that is the grand, completed record of volunteer service in behalf of a redeemed Union, and in securing the freedom of every slave on American soil. This fact is more eloquent than any words can possibly be, so I shall not attempt the impossible by striving to add to its surpassing grandeur and glory.

David S. Coddington declared during our war that "our greatest General was our General Greatness," and in the prospect of the future this truth must be kept in mind. We are living in the closing years of the greatest century in the life of man; and our nation which was feeble in resources and comparatively few in numbers at its opening in the year 1800, will be "great, glorious and free" in 1900. From 5,000,000 souls we will have increased to 80,000,000 during this wonderful period in the world's history. Amazing progress from every point of view. Along moral and industrial lines we are the wonder of older nations. The mind would stagger under a recital of the commerce, internal and external, which is annually moved by our avenues of transportation, and of the output of all our industries. This is not the occasion for full details of this character, but the fruits of our peaceful era have their seedtime in part in the travail of the nation when these flags were first placed within the keeping of Oneida County volunteers.

CONCLUSION.

Thus, comrades and friends, I have spoken from a full heart, to the best of my ability, concerning several important questions and sentiments which seemed to me worthy of consideration at this historic meeting. I have fallen far short of what I desired to present for your consideration, but it is always true that the inspiration which move enc in contemplation are greater than any spoken words.

These flags, respectively carried by the 14th, 26th, 97th, 117th, 146th Infantry Regiments, the 2d Heavy Artillery, and the 3d Light Artillery, N. Y. S. V., constitute new treasures for this worthy Memorial and Historical Building. It will not be long before the precious souvenirs of Grand Army Posts will also be gathered into similar repositories for safe-keeping in all of the States where such posts are located. The sure harvest of death is fast decimating the ranks of our noble order, and very soon these precious flags alone will remain to view as the dear objects which departed veterans loved so well and cherished so fondly.

The battles of the war were all long since ended, while the

battle of life daily confronts us all. It is for each veteran to so live as to prove worthy of the service he rendered his country in war in the nobler battles of a good life work in peace. Heroes are needed in time of peace as well as in periods of war. The still, small voice of duty demands brave actions in ever increasing numbers, and to live right, in the uplifting associations of manly virtues, in all good words and works, constitutes true heroism and nobility of character.

When these flags are placed on easy view let the children come at least once a year and look with uncovered heads upon them—mute, but eloquent in their silence, and thus receive safe inspirations of patriotism and love of country. Let the "Stars and Stripes" become a treasure in every home, in every place of business, and in ever church; display it over every school-house, and make it the chief ornament at every private and public function everywhere within our borders. If we love and cherish it at home, the world will respect and honor it abroad. Let it become a universal monument of a "more perfect Union;" and under its folds let freedom ring out, from the centre all round to the seas, the glad sentiment, one Flag, one Country and one National Destiny.

Let every public meeting, outside of church services, close by singing "America," and thus fix in the heart of hearts of all our people the safe and sweet sentiments of appreciative national patriotism.

Comrades: When the final taps are sounded and our days on earth are ended, may we all pass within the vail, leaving seeds of loyalty and love of liberty behind us that will take root in young hearts, and thus add to the great heritage of liberty saving elements of Christian citizenship, happy safeguards, equal to all the dangers and needs of future generations.

> "To the hero, when his sword
> Has won the battle for the free,
> Death's voice sounds like a prophets' word;
> And in its hollow tones are heard
> The thanks of millions yet to be!"

J. B. Jones proposed three cheers for the next Commander-in-Chief of the G. A. R., and they were given with great heartiness.

President Proctor then introduced Mrs. Louise Cooper Graham-Schantz, who wrote the letter presenting the flag of the 117th Regiment. Many of the comrades came forward and shook hands with her. Commander Shaw proposed three cheers for the lady, which were given.

The exercises closed with the singing of "America." The boys then repaired to the adjoining room and saw the flags deposited in a place of safe keeping.

[From the *Utica Daily Press*, December 15, 1897.]

The Flags Presented.

Yesterday's flag presentation at the Munson-Williams Memorial Building was an occasion of unusual interest. The arrangements were perfect and carried out faultlessly. The addresses were timely, instructive and entertaining by men of prominence and ability. Not less deserving were many whose formal part was perhaps not so large, but whose interest in the banners was as intense, the men who followed where they led, who bore brave freemen's part in the fight which preserved the Union. They came from various points scattered through Central New York and took pride in the occasion. It was a notable gathering as well as a notable event. Commander Shaw, at the head of the State Department of the Grand Army of the Republic, honored the day with his presence and added to it by his excellent oration. General Curtis, familiarly known as the "Hero of Fort Fisher," told the story of that famous battle as only he could tell it. To T. R. Proctor much of the splendid success of yesterday's ceremonies is due, for his was the guiding hand, and what he undertakes never fails of realizing the fullest expectation. His thoughtful attention and courteous hospitality were features greatly appreciated.

Yesterday's flag presentation might have been more appropriately called flag preservation. They are now in safe keeping where for years and years to come no harm shall touch them, no negligence befall them and where time's aging influence will be reduced to the minimum. Securely encased and carefully guarded, they will remain the emblems of a country's patriotism long after those who bore and those who followed them have fought their last fight and gone to their long home. It is eminently fitting that these flags should be gathered together under one roof where all can see them and feel that they are safe from loss or accidental destruction. No better place could be found for them, none more appropriate, none more reliable and secure. There has been no change of proprietorship only of location. The veterans are proud and pleased that the banners they bore so well have found so permanent and appropriate a home. There they will be an inspiration to thousands, who looking at the worn and tattered standards will be prompted to recall what they represent and to revere the memory of those who used them in the trying times of civil war. No other section sent braver or more loyal soldiers to the front than this and no honors are too great to bestow upon them. It was a happy thought which suggested bringing all these old flags together, as has been done. No better or worthier disposition could have been made of them. A part of this country's history, they will be sacredly kept by the Oneida Historical Society in its splendid Munson-Williams Memorial Building. Yesterday was a red letter day in the calendar of the local veterans, one long to be pleasantly remembered.

[From the *Utica Observer*, December 15, 1897.]

In the Munson-Williams Memorial.

Yesterday was a day which will never be forgotten by any who participated in the events within the walls of the Munson-Williams Memorial. The war flags and the trophies of the

Oneida County Regiments in the war of the rebellion were then and there formally, and with heartfelt words, placed in the custody of the Oneida Historical Society to be held in sacred keeping "beyond the touch, but in sight of all who may wish to see them," as Mr. Proctor felicitously expressed it. And, by the way, when his touching address accepting the trust on behalf of the Society was ended, and tear-wet veterans arose as one with mighty cheers for him, there was no doubt remaining that these colors were now in a better custody than ever before they had been—though they came from loving hands.

Col. Shaw, the orator of the day, was right when he said with broken voice that none present would ever look on such a scene again. The stoutest hearts were melted by the incidents of the afternoon.

"The bravest are the tenderest."

Col. Shaw was himself so affected by the spirit of the occasion that his address, which thousands read in type last evening, was delivered with an eloquence and earnestness which deeply impressed every listener.

The tribute paid in the evening to Gen. Curtis, "the Hero of Fort Fisher," by the full attendance despite the driving storm, was one of which the speaker was eminently worthy. And "The Story of Fort Fisher" was well worth hearing. Its effect was heightened when he was able to point to soldiers in the audience, men of the 117th, who were with him in the fight and to tell of their individual deeds. The whole story was told with the dignity of a statesman and the modesty of a hero.

Yesterday's events fully doubled the numbers of the friends of the Oneida Historical Society, and the home of the Society will hereafter have a new and inspiring interest. Mr. Proctor has not often presented a better idea than that which was successfully carried out yesterday.

GEN. N. M. CURTIS.

Address of General N. M. Curtis.

In the evening the auditorium of the Munson-Williams Memorial was filled with Grand Army men and their wives, and members of the Society. General Curtis was greeted with hearty applause as he entered the hall with Thomas R. Proctor, the Vice President of the Society.

Mr. Proctor introduced General Curtis with these words: "Ladies and gentlemen—it requires but four words to introduce of the lecturer of the evening, 'the Hero of Fort Fisher.'"

General Curtis spoke for an hour and a half, illustrating his lecture by a large wall map. His graphic story of the battle in which he bore so prominent a part aroused the patriotism of his audience. Relating to the first expedition he said in part:

At the first interview between General Grant and Admiral Porter, the admiral objected to the selection of General Butler to command the army forces. At this interview Weitzel was agreed upon. General Grant directed General Butler to send General Weitzel down to reconnoiter Fort Fisher. General Grant states in forwarding Butler's report of January 3, 1865, that "my orders to General Butler to prepare it were given verbally, to avoid publicity of the time of sailing and destination." December 6, 1864, in writing instructions to General Butler General Grant stated: "The first object of the expedition under General Weitzel is to close to the enemy the port of Wilmington. * * * The object of the expedition will be gained by effecting a landing on the mainland between Cape Fear River and the Atlantic north of the north entrance to the river. Should such landing be effected whilst the enemy still hold Fort Fisher and the batteries guarding the entrance to the river, then the troops should entrench themselves and by co-operating with the navy effect the reduction and capture of those pieces." General Butler, at 10 P. M., December 24, 1864, wrote Admiral Porter:

"We will endeavor to effect a landing above Flag Pond Hill battery, between that and Half Moon, at such an hour as may be fixed upon by consultation between yourself and General Weitzel, who will have command of the troops, and who will meet you at any hour you choose to arrange details. * * * I design, in the first place, to send on shore a party of reconnoissance sufficiently strong to hold the landing if we gain a good hold, and then to land as rapidly as possible our whole force, and if from the reconnoissance it is deemed practicable to attempt an assault on Fort Fisher the assault will be made."

Under the plans agreed upon between General Weitzel and Admiral Porter, I was detailed to land with 500 of my brigade by row boats supplied by the navy, in charge of Lieutenant (now Commodore) Farquier. Having got my men in the boats formed in line with a launch carrying a howitzer on each flank, I directed them to maintain their alignment and reach the shore as soon as possible; at the same time requesting the Lieutenant to put me on the beach in advance of the line. About this time I saw a boat pass the right of my line headed for the shore. I asked that I be landed first. My crew were the better oarsmen and I landed and carried Captain Glisson's flag, taken from the gig, to the sand dunes before our competitors reached the shore. The boat brought General Weitzel. He congratulated me on winning the race and said, "I had offered $1,000 to beat your boat." I said the difference between a boats crew from a transport and one from a United States man-of-war was more than $1,000, and that all I had to do was to request the officer in charge to land me first. As soon as the troops landed and formed in line, pickets were thrown out to the north and west, and flankers as we moved down the beach. Soon after we started Captain Koonts, Company A, 42d North Carolina Infantry, occupying Flag Pond Battery, half a mile south of our landing, raised a white flag, indicating his desire to surrender, and his command of sixty-seven men and officers were taken off by boats from the naval vessels. The log book of the Santiago de Cuba, of December 25, 1864, states that we took possession of Flag Pond Battery at 3 P. M. We then marched down the beach about one mile south of Flag Pond Battery and halted. General Weitzel made a careful examination of Fort Fisher and its surroundings and stated the fort was not injured by the navy fire—only one gun displaced—and requested me to take his glass and report how I found it. I looked and agreed with him as to the physical condition of the work. We were at that time about one and one-half miles north of Fort Fisher. General Weitzel says in his report; "I proceeded in person, accompanying the 142d New York, to within about 800 yards of Fort Fisher, a point from which I had a good view of the work. From what I saw there and before that time, and from what I had heard from what I considered reliable sources, I believe the work to be a square bastioned work; it has a high relief, a wide and deep ditch, excepting on the sea front, a glacis, has casemates and bomb-proofs sufficiently large to hold its garrison. * * * * I returned, as directed, to the Major General commanding, found him on the gunboat Chamberlain within easy range and good view of the work, and frankly reported to him that it would be butchery to order an assault on that work under the circumstances, After examining it himself carefully, he came to the same conclusion, and directed the troops to be re-embarked."

General Weitzel makes no mention of the orders given me

when he left to report to General Butler, but in his testimony before the Committee on the Conduct of the War, page 76, he says: "After I had made a reconnoissance, I returned, as I had been directed, to General Butler, to make my report. I directed General Curtis to remain in command, and to push on towards the work until he was stopped, and to find out what was there; and if he discovered anything new to immediately report it to General Butler, and I left a signal sergeant with him for that purpose."

It was probably about 3.30 P. M. when General Weitzel left me to report to General Butler. The signal sergeant did not remain with me. In General Butler's testimony before the Committee on Conduct of the War, page 23, he says: "Gen. Weitzel stated that he thought it was impossible to assault the fort successfully. Being unwilling to leave the matter without trying, and seeing from the state of the weather that it must be an assault or nothing, I said to Col. Comstock, who was on board with me, 'Jump into a boat with Gen. Weitzel, (Col. R. H. Jackson, not Gen. Weitzel, went with Col. Comstock,) pull ashore, and examine with General Weitzel, (Colonel Jackson) and report to me if an assault is feasible; to me it does not look possible, but I am unwilling to give up.' I had a vivid perception of the future which has overtaken me. They went on shore. The surf had begun to rise, so that they got very wet in landing. At the same time General Graham reported to me. He said: 'General, you have got either to provide for those troops to-night on shore some way, or get them off, because it is getting so rough that we cannot land much longer.' * * * * * * Considering a few moments, I determined the course of action that should govern me."

All this must have occurred before 4 P. M., Capt. James Alden, commanding the U. S. S. Brooklyn, reports: * * * "At 4 o'clock, just two hours after the landing commenced, the general commanding came alongside of this ship and said: 'It has become necessary to re-embark the troops; will you send your boats to assist?' You can judge of my surprise at the turn affairs had taken, for at that moment everything seemed propitious, the bombardment was at its hight, little or no surf on the beach, and no serious indications of bad weather."

The reconnoitering party effected a landing at 2.10 P. M., and was followed by all the second division and one regiment of colored troops, (about 4,000 men,) before the order to re-embark was given by General Butler. All remained on the beach near the point of landing excepting a portion of the first brigade. At four o'clock, when the order was given to re-embark a detachment of the reconnoitering party had reached Craig's Landing, and Lieutenant Simpson cut the telegraph wire, thus breaking communication between the fort and Willmington. The skirmish line was approaching the fort, and less than half a mile away. At 4.20, when a navy shot cut the garrison flag-staff, the skirmishers were at the stockade, and Lieutenant Walling in command, went through the ditch, stockade, up the parapet, and brought the flag away. He presented it to me at the bank of the ditch. I immediately sent an officer to the reserve and directed them to immediately come down to the earthwork at Cape Fear River about 800 yards north of the flank of the fort, and then go up the beach and report to General Butler that we had cut the telegraph line, breaking communication with Willmington, and captured the garrison flag, which I was about to take to the beach and exhibit to the navy that they might direct their fire in support of any subsequent movements we should make. Two musket shots were directed at the party carrying the flag to the beach. They went over us. Quite high shots you can see, in order to go over the head of one of the party. After reaching the beach, and seeing no movement on the part of the reserve, I went up to ascertain the failure to comply with my order to advance, and was then imformed that a short time before the receipt of my order an order had been received from the commanding general to retire up the beach, and that it had been sent to me at the western end of the line, and in view of the fact that it was an order from my superior, my own order being directly contrary to that from headquarters, had been held in abeyance until I should be made aware of the nature of the order of the commanding general. This order was probably received at the reserve about the time the flag was captured. Notwithstanding the order to retire, I took such of my brigade as had come up and moved down to the earthwork before mentioned; some 800 yards from the fort, sending the 117th regiment up the Wilmington road running near the Cape Fear River with orders to advance a mile if they could do so without resistance from the enemy, and to establish a picket line to extend from the Cape Fear River across the peninsula to the flankers we had already thrown out when we marched down the beach. In making this movement, Captain Stevens, with two men, went in advance of the regiment as skirmishers to prevent its falling into an ambush, and when they had advanced a little to the north of Craig's Landing Major Reese, of the North Carolina Junior Reserves, stepped into the road, threw up his hands and surrendered before a shot had been fired or the regiment had arrived in sight. A portion of his command escaped, but some 230 officers and men were brought in and finally sent north. The regiment at the same time captured two guns of a light battery and six caissons. A courier carrying a message out of the fort was shot and his horse taken only a short distance from the parapet. At the conclusions of these operations a second order was received directing me to retire. To this I sent in reply a communication stating what had been accomplished subsequently to my first report, stating there was no enemy in sight and that no resistance had been offered beyond the two musket shots fired at the party carrying the flag to the beach, and I should hold his order in abeyance until the commanding general could become acquainted with the defenseless condition of the work. Soon after this, at dark, Colonel Comstock and Colonel Jackson came to this out-work, closely followed by the division commander. To them a detailed statement was made of the operations of the reconnoitering party up to the time of their arrival, and they were requested to notify General Butler, that in my opinion the fort could be successfully assaulted the next morning, one hour after the navy should open fire. Neither of these officers would assume any responsibility as to my failure to comply with the orders to retire, but General Ames stated, "If you feel confident that you can capture the fort you ought to make the attempt with the men you have at your disposal." I stated that it was then dark and the navy was retiring, and as it retired the enemy would come out from their bombproofs and man their guns and would slaughter me should I then attempt an assault without the protection of the naval fire, and that I could not assault until daylight and the navy should keep the enemy in their bombproofs. These officers returned. Colonel Comstock, as I believed from what he said, intended to advise General Butler to prepare for an assault the next morning. One hour after this I received the third order to retire, which I complied with by withdrawing my skirmishers from the fort and pickets from the Wilmington road, and with our prisoners marched up the beach to the point of debarkation. There I found that the troops which had landed and remained on the beach in that vicinity had all re-embarked. I got off a portion of my command and the commissioned confederate officers, when the surf became so high the boats could not live, as stated by those in command of them. Between six and seven hundred of my command and two hundred and thirty prisoners remained on shore until we were taken off on the following Tuesday afternoon.

* * * * * * *

From an examination of the chronological order of events, as they transpired from 2.10 P. M. until 4 P.M., it will be seen that about two-thirds of General Butler's command effected a landing on the beach, and that no report from the reconnoitering party, which had been sent to the front with orders "to report anything that might be discovered to General Butler," had been received by him. He had acted solely on his own judgment and the advice of General Weitzel not to assault based on the information obtained from the observation made of the fort at a distance of a mile and a half—a distance so great that he could not see its formation, as is evidenced by his report, in which he states that "it was a square bastioned fort, with casemates and a glacis." It really had one bastion, no casemates and no glacis. General Butler did not wait to receive a report of the discoveries made by the reconnoitering party, and failed to wait for a report from Colonel Comstock and Colonel Jackson, who were sent ashore to specially ascertain if in their opinion "an assault was feasible." The opinion of General Weitzel not to assault the work was made in absolute ignorance of the orders to General Butler, wherein it was stated "the object of the expedition will be gained by effecting a landing on the mainland between Cape Fear River and the Atlantic north of the north entrance to the river."

* * * * * * *

General Butler telegraphed at 8 P. M., December 27, 1864, to General Grant, announcing the return of the expedition to Fortress Monroe, and gave a brief summary of the events attending it. At 5.30 P. M., December 28, President Lincoln telegraphed General Grant as follows:

"If there be no objections please tell me what you now understand of the Wilmington expedition, present and prospective." To which General Grant replied. at 8.30 P. M.: "The Wilmington expedition has proven a gross and culpable failure. Many of the troops are now back here. Delays and free talk of the object of the expedition enabled the enemy to move troops to Wilmington to defeat it. After the expedition sailed from Fortress Monroe three days of fine weather was squandered, during which the enemy was without a force to protect himself. Who is to blame I hope will be known."

* * * * * *

The morning of the 29th of December, the transport upon which I returned from Fort Fisher dropped anchor in Hampton Roads, I went on shore for breakfast and was sent for by Gen. Grant and questioned as to what I saw and did after landing at Fort Fisher. I gave him a detailed account of the operations of my command while on shore, and a description of the fort. He stated that my description differed from that of other officers, who reported it as a "square bastioned work with casemates and glacis, and its exterior sides averaging about 200 yards." I replied that I had been within a few yards of it and knew it had no casemates, no glacis and only one bastioned angle, and that its land face was about half a mile long, and its sea face over a mile long; no parapet on the south or west. He said the expedition ought not to have failed and that he might desire to hear further from me. I returned to my ship to wait for other transports to come in before we should proceed up the river.

In a few hours after I left General Grant I received a telegram from General Weitzel to report at once to his headquarters. I went up in advance of my troops, and when I reached General Weitzel's headquarters he said he had sent for me in obedience to a telegram from General Grant, who wanted a detailed account of what I and the officers of my command who were nearest the fort had seen. I sent for Captain Walling, 142 New York, who brought the garrison flag from the fort, Lieutenant George Simpson, 142d New York, who cut the telegraph wire, and Lieutenant G. W. Ross, 117th New York, John W. White, James Spring and Henry Blair of the 142d New York Volunteers, who were on the skirmish line. The statements of these officers and men were taken down and sent to General Grant, through Colonel Comstock. General Grant forwarded them to the Secretary of War "with the request that these papers be filed with Major-General Butler's report of the expedition against Fort Fisher, N. C., as statements appended to said report by me. I should have appended them when I forwarded the report, but Lieutenant-Colonel Comstock, aide-de-camp, to whom they were made, was absent on the second expedition against the fort and had them with him. These statements of the officers and men named were reduced to writing immediately after the return of the unsuccessful expedition against Fort Fisher, and were handed to Colonel Comstock about the 2d day of January, 1865. General Butler, before ordering re-embarkation and return of the expedition he assumed to command, might have had within information, and it was his duty, before giving such orders, to have known the results of the reconnoissance, which could have been most satisfactorily learned from those most in advance."

These quotations from the official records plainly show who it was that disregarded the instructions of General Grant and was responsible for the failure of the first expedition.

Some careless readers have asserted that the inquiry ordered by the Senate, January 12, 1865: "Resolved, That the committee on the conduct of the war be directed to inquire into the causes of the failure of the late expedition against Wilmington, North Carolina, and to report the facts to the Senate," fully acquits General Butler of the responsibility charged by General Grant.

A careful reading of the evidence taken by that committee will show that the order of the Senate was not complied with. The inquiry was made not to ascertain the causes of the failure, but as to the propriety of assaulting the fort, as the findings of the committee clearly show: "In conclusion, your committee would say, from all the testimony before them, that the determination of General Butler not to assault the fort seems to have been fully justified by all the facts and circumstances then known or afterwards ascertained."

The result of the second expedition fully corroborates the correctness of the description of the works on Federal Point given by myself and members of my command, who were the only persons within 800 yards of the main work, and justified our opinion that the fort could have been captured on the first expedition had the commanding general complied with General Grant's orders and intelligently attempted to have carried out the plans he announced to Admiral Porter the night before the landing. The reason given for refusing to carry out those plans were not justified by the circumstances and conditions then existing. To the first claim that the troops on shore were without provisions or ammunition, it needs only to be stated that ample supplies of both for thirty days could have been landed in one-half the time given to re-embarking the troops— about 3,500—which were taken off that night. To the claim that the troops on shore could not maintain their position against the large force of the enemy in their front, he had the assurance of Admiral Porter that the fleet could hold the position and give them complete protection. The opinion of

Admiral Porter was supported by the fact that not one of the naval vessels left the station, nor did one of the frail transports waiting to carry the troops north leave its anchorage in front of the beach until all the stranded troops were taken on board Tuesday afternoon.

* * * * * * *

Colonel William Lamb commanded the fort two years and a half. He found it an unfinished work with four guns, which he said " the frigate Minnesota could have destroyed the works and driven us out in a few hours." He made it during his occupation the largest and best equipped fortification constructed by the confederates.

He says in his article—" The Defense of Fort Fisher "—Battles and Leaders of the War, Vol. 4, page 642 :

" Fort Fisher commanded the last gateway between the confederate states and the outside world. Its capture, with the resulting loss of all the Cape Fear River defenses, and of Wilmington, the great importing depot of the south, effectually ended all blockade-running. Lee sent me word that Fort Fisher must be held or he could not subsist his army."

Another author relates a specific transaction which he completed between the time of the failure of the first and the arrival of the second expedition to Fort Fisher. Thomas E. Taylor, an Englishman, who took a prominent part in blockade-running, says, page 139 of his book, " Running the Blockade ":

" That morning I had an appointment with the Commissary General, (this was in Richmond, Va., in December, 1864,) who divulged to me, under promise of secrecy, that Lee's army was in terrible straits, and had in fact rations for only thirty days. He asked me if I could help him. I said I would do my best, and after some negotiations he undertook to pay me a profit of 350 per cent. upon any provisions and meat I could bring in within the next three weeks.   *   *   *   Although it was a hard trip, it paid well, as we had on board coming out a most magnificent cargo, a great deal of sea island cotton, the profits upon which and the provisions I had taken in amounted to over eighty-five thousand pounds—not bad work for about twenty days."

The day of the capture of Fort Fisher, January 15, 1865, he wrote to his chiefs in Liverpool, England : (p. 136, same vol.)

"Altogether I think the confederate government is going to the bad, and if they don't take care the confederacy will go too. I never saw things look so gloomy, and I think spring will finish them unless they make a change for the better. Georgia is gone, and they say Sherman is going to seize Branchville; if he does Charleston and Wilmington will be done—and if Wilmington goes Lee has to evacuate Richmond and retire into Tennessee. He told me the other day that if they did not keep Wilmington he could not save Richmond. They nearly had Fort Fisher—they were within sixty yards of it—and had they pushed on as they ought to have done, could have taken it. It was a terrible bombardment; they estimate that about 40,000 shells were sent into it. Colonel Lamb behaved like a brick—splendidly. I got the last of the Whitworths in, and they are now at the fort. They are very hard up for food in the field, but the Banshee has this time 600 barrels of pork and 1,500 boxes of meat—enough to feed Lee's army for a month."

Second Expedition.

Early Friday morning, the 13th of January, under cover of the naval vessels, the transports stood in shore and began the landing of the troops, which was effected at 3 p. m., together with the landing of extra rations, ammunition and intrenching tools. The landing was made through a heavy surf, in which much of the provisions in haversacks and ammunition in boxes were thoroughly soaked.

A line was established across the peninsula in the early evening, but soon abandoned for a second line, a mile further south, on which breastworks were thrown up during the night and completed by 8 A. M., extending from the beach to Cape Fear river. The First Brigade was on the right of this line until the morning of the 14th, when it was withdrawn, and General Terry directed its commander to report to him until otherwise ordered. The brigade, under his instructions, then marched to Battery Holland, below Craig's Landing—accompanying General Terry and Colonel Comstock. Going down, a shell from the rebel gun-boat Chickamauga exploded near the head of the column, seriously wounding Captain J. H. Reeve, commanding 3d N. Y., and three men of that regiment.

* * * * * * *

Before advancing to the first line every officer and man had been instructed as to his movements and the order in which they would take place, and that the point of attack was between the first and second traverse.

Three short advances were made, during which the confederate infantry would come to the parapet, but when the line halted they would return to the bomb-proofs; each time remaining longer at the parapet and suffering greater damage from the naval fire. When the enemy seemed determined to remain on the parapet, the final rush was made. The commander of the line called aloud "forward," advancing as he arose from the ground. Each officer and soldier had been instructed to advance as he arose from the ground, by which means the first volley passed over their heads, doing but little damage. They were fifteen paces to the front before they had assumed the usual altitude of a running man, which is about one-third less than the standing altitude. Although the navy fire had made many openings in the stockade, one hundred axes had been distributed in the brigade, and much chopping had to be done to enable the men to get through to ascend the parapet and contend for the ground between the first and second traverses. It was done; and a marker of the right regiment—the 117th N. Y., under command of Lieut. Col. F. X. Meyer—placed on the second traverse. Its right to remain there was tested in a hand to hand contest, in which the Yankees won. The next move was to go down to the terreplain and surround the men, serving a Napoleon gun at the gate, and a number of infantry posted at the stockade west of the gate. Their capture removed the chief obstacle to an approach by the road, and some of the second brigade entered the fort through the gate. A number came to the parapet and advanced with the first brigade, sharply contending at each of the traverses. Colonel Moore, 203d Pennsylvania, was killed soon after mounting the parapet with the colors of his regiment in his hands. Colonel Pennypacker was wounded at the third traverse and carried to the rear.

* * * * * * *

At no time did I see an officer or man evading his duty—officers of all ranks and men vied with one another in their efforts to capture the fort. The men of each brigade, after entering the fort, fought side by side on the parapet or on the floor of the fort. Officers fought with muskets, not for the purpose of inspiring the men, but as a practical contribution to the force of the assailants.

* * * * * * *

Admiral Porter wanted success no less than General Terry,

and was ready to take any step in the line of his profession to win it. He knew, as all did, that a naval column would divert the garrison, and asked the navy to furnish the men to form it. In the pursuit of victory desperate chances are often taken. Never did men undertake a more difficult or hazardous task, and never did men offer themselves to their country's cause with more zeal, courage or unselfish devotion than did the officers and men of the navy and marines on the beach at Fort Fisher. Their action contributed to the progress of the army—whether the gain justified the losses we shall never know. The naval column was important as a diversion, but its value was slight in comparison with the fire of the six hundred guns trained on the fort. The fleet maintained an uninterrupted fire for two days, exceeding in effectivensss any bombardment recorded in the annals of war. To Admiral Porter's fleet the army was indebted for an uncontested landing, uninterrupted approach to within charging distance of the fort, and to its well directed fire in advance of the assaulting lines for a success, which, without the navy's aid, would have been impossible.

*   *   *   *   *   *   *

It will not, I trust, be out of place to refer to the enemy and their defense of the fort.

The constant fire of the navy for two days deprived the garrison of the opportunity to rest or prepare food. While they suffered little from the naval fire until the advance of the assaulting lines brought them out of their bomb-proofs, they then came under the hottest fire men ever encountered. Colonel Lamb skillfully managed the defense, aided by the valuable services of General Whiting. They protected their men until the decisive moment, and then led them with conspicuous gallantry.

The left of the parapet was in charge of a junior officer whose mistake, that of a moment only, was in failing to mount the parapet and contest our advance from the ditch; although in doing so he would have faced the terrible fire of the navy. The men serving the piece of artillery covering the road, west of the parapet, were so intent in serving their gun that they were seized in the act of loading it, by men of the 117th N. Y., who went down from the parapet after capturing the enemy resisting us between the first and second traverses.

* * * * * * *

There were probably 5,000 men brought into action. There are no records in the War Department giving the number of officers and men by brigades, of the second division, or the number of men taken into action. It is estimated that the first (Curtis') brigade numbered 900 officers and men; the second (Pennypacker's) brigade 1,700 officers and men; the third (Bell's) brigade 1,100 officers and men; second (Abbott's) brigade, first division, 1,300 officers and men.

The return of casualties in the United States forces engaged in the storming of Fort Fisher, N. C., January 15, 1865, is as follows:

(W. R., Ser, 95, Page 405.)

	Estimated No. Engaged.	Killed. Officers.	Men.	Wounded. Officers.	Men.	Missing.
Curtis,	900	2	37	18	166	5
Pennypacker,	1,700	6	45	16	211	2
Bell,	1,100	2	14	6	91	2
Abbott,	1,300		4	2	21	4
Staff,				5		
Grand Total,	5,000	10	100	47	489	13

The missing include those injured beyond recognition, and those buried in the sand by the explosion of a magazine after the capture.

References to the Personnel of the 117th.

The neighbors of the 117th New York should know that in the distribution of honors for valiant services and unyielding endurance under one of the hottest fires men were ever called upon to meet that none stood in advance of the members of that organization. Lieutenant-Colonel Meyer and Major Bagg were wounded early in battle, yet neither faltered while able to stand, and each manfully struggled to be foremost in the advance.

Captain D. B. Magill conducted the advance over the eighth traverse, and lost a leg in carrying it. Captain A. E. Smith (later killed with Custer fighting Indians) on General Terry's staff, although wounded, carried orders to the end. I saw Lieutenant Skinner and another officer nursing wounds, yet pressing forward, generously giving more attention to the enemy than themselves. Corporal J. B. Jones, of the color guard, carried messages to different parts of the line, intelligently performing the duties of a staff officer.

Exhibitions of extraordinary acts of personal courage were shown by officers and men whose names should be mentioned in a more detailed account. It is no common thing for men to stay in line after being wounded, yet there were cases where men carrying the most effective arms in the war—a good musket properly handled, unable to stand on their feet by exhaustion from wounds, in a sitting position, loaded their pieces for others to fire them. Whatever credit be given to officers for the plan of attack and directing the movements it must not be forgotten that there were hundreds with muskets as well as swords entitled to the highest commendation.

I had an opportunity to see much of the 4th Oneida from the Spring of 1863, at Suffolk, until disabled in this battle. It was at all times a fine organization, yet I believe it was brought to its highest state of efficiency while under command of Colonel Rufus Daggett, seconded by field and company officers of marked ability. Their promotions were worthily earned, and they justly merit the high commendation bestowed upon them.

twenty-five voices, led by E. L. Griffiths. It sang with excellent harmony and great heartiness. Its music was inspiring.

Rev. J. V. Ferguson, Chaplain of the Ninety-Seventh regiment, offered prayer.

The two flags, one an American flag presented to the regiment by the ladies of Boonville, and the other the coat of arms of the Empire State, very finely embroidered and inscribed "Conkling Rifles," were then presented to the society by John H. Merriman of Whitestown, formerly of Company D, and Arch B. Snow of Boonville.

Mr. Merriman said: This evening is one of unusual pleasure to those who fought together under this flag. At the time the other regimental flags were presented this flag was out on the skirmish line somewhere, but it got home at last. Thank God for it. I will not attempt to give you a historical record of it; but if you can decipher hieroglyphics, you will see where it has been punctuated by the blood of 181 veterans who fell under it. You will find in its folds a chapter as grand as any you have ever read in English history. This flag, placed in the archives of this hall, will stand not only as a memento of what has been achieved, but it will increase the patriotism of the rising generation. The flag is not in the condition it once was. It is hardly recognizable. But its folds are eloquent testimony of the patriotism of the men who fought under it. They speak of sad hearts—— (Here the speaker's voice became choked with tears, and it was some minutes before he could continue.) He then said: My heart is too full for me to express all the emotions which the sight of that old flag awakens. I will now present the flag to the Oneida Historical Society, to be placed where it can be seen by the rising generation as an emblem of all we love and cherish. May God bless you and us. (Applause.)

Captain Arch B. Snow of Boonville presented the Conkling flag. He said:

Mr. President and members of the Oneida Historical Society: From information secured from newspaper report, I had no thought that the flags of the 97th New York Volunteers were to be formally presented to your honorable society to-day, and the first reliable information on the subject I read in this morning's paper while on my way hither. I assure you that I most sincerely and heartily regret that the few concluding words that formally consign these historic relics to your custody, had not been delegated to an abler and worthier tongue than mine. The time upon which this ceremony falls is most auspicious. War, battle and victory is the theme of daily conversation. The national ensign proudly floating in the beeeze meets the eye on every hand, and this is the anniversary of the battle month of the war of the rebellion. Thirty-four years ago General Sedgwick was killed. Thirty-four years ago to-day the 97th regiment, after five days of constant fighting, got the first chance to cook coffee, and thirty-four years ago to-morrow General Grant sent the historic dispatch to the war department which contained the famous line, now thrilling and momentious in its import: "I propose to fight it out on this line if it takes all summer." (Applause.) The boys who with rosy cheecks, springing step and patriotic enthusiasm, responded to the call of country; the counterparts of those who to-day go forth to fight the Spaniard; have long since passed the divide which separates youth from middle life, and the surviving few are now sturdily marching down the sunset slope of life. A few more years and their persons, their deeds, even their names will be but a memory. It is most fitting, therefore, that the battle flags, the visible emblems and evidence of their imperishable deeds, should with fitting ceremonies be deposited in places of safe deposit trom the corroding touch of time, and the destroying clutch of the relic hunter. That they have not been thus secure while in the custody of the State, the absence of the beautiful lancewood staff of the Conkling flag is now in evidence. These two flags are historic. The Conkling flag, embroidered in part by the hands of the wife of Senator Conkling, and presented through Colonel Wheelock to the 97th regiment shortly after the battle of Fredericksburg, from that time forward floated on every battlefield in which the Army of the Potomac was engaged till the surrender at Appomatox. The old battle flag, now a tattered rag, with broken, splintered, patched and mended staff, was presented to the regiment by the patriotic ladies of the village of Boonville in December, 1861. The president of the ladies' fair association which raised the money for its purchase by God's grace and mercy, is spared in health and strength to-day to grace this ceremony with her presence. The eyes of the great majority of those who saw it floating in battle smoke when fresh and bright, and new, are now closed forever; and the eyes of those who now survive are growing dim with age. We are admonished, therefore, that the time approaches when the last of the soldiers of the great rebellion will be gone. Oneida county has the unique distinction of having furnished five regiments in the war of the rebellion, three of which are numbered among the "three hundred fighting regiments of the war," and the county that furnished to the councils of the nation a Kernan and a Conkling, to the warriors of the nation a McQuade, a Jenkins, a Wheelock and a Butterfield, through the generous munificence of its citizens furnishes also a place of deposit, magnificent and secure, where our children's children, for generations yet to come, may look with patriotic reverence upon the visible evidence of the valor and devotion of those who have gone before. (Applause.)

The lady referred to by Captain Snow was Mrs. L. C. Childs, of Utica, who was present.

In accepting the flag President Proctor said:

Men and Women—Comrades: When the battle flags of the 14th, 26th, 117th and 146th regiments, that of the Second New York Heavy Artillery, General McQuade's headquarters flag and several others, some of which were captured in battle, were placed in charge of this society in December last, it was but natural that the survivors of the 97th regiment were disappointed that they could not be represented, but their flags were in the capitol at Albany. It was thought that an application to the adjutant general, or if not to him then to the governor or the State, would be all sufficient to cause the flags to be restored to the survivors of the regiment. They were, however, informed that it would be necessary to have an act of the Legislature authorizing their restoration, and this was accomplished through the efforts of Assemblyman Williams and Senator Coggeshall, to whom the veterans as well as this society feel very grateful.

It was supposed that his excellency the governor would not hesitate to sign this bill, but objection was raised that it was a dangerous precedent, and that other regiments would want their flags. These objections were overcome, however, by the persuasive influence of Colonel Griffith, the governor's private secretary, Congressman Sherman, always the friend of the veteran, and Colonel Shaw, the department commander of the G. A. R.

It is said that great men sometimes change their minds, but that fools never do. Let us be thankful that our governor was great enough to change his mind, and that his gracious act has restored these precious treasures to their rightful owners. It is but fair to tell you that the efforts of the distinguished gentlemen just referred to was secured largely by the untiring exertion of Colonel Merriman, the president of the 97th Regiment Association. It was his earnestness that inspired the co-operation of others, and it is pleasant to remember the occasion when with moist eyes he exclaimed that it would be the happiest day of his life when these flags were returned to those who had the greatest claim on them—the men who had fought under their folds. Colonel Merriman, your comrades and friends salute you and congratulate you. (Applause.)

The Oneida Historical Society accepts the care of these flags, and will place them with those of the other Oneida county regiments, and they will remain in this building to tell the present and future generations of the valor and patriotism of Oneida's sons.

It is but right and proper that at a meeting of this kind some allusion should be made to the brave young men who left this city to do battle if need be for the nation only last week. (Applause.) They turned their backs upon comfortable homes, and with their faces toward the enemy stepped out into the unknown. It seems now as though they may never be called upon to face the horrors of war, and let us hope and pray that they will not, but they are entitled to just as much credit as if they actually fought for their country, because they have shown by their action that they were able and willing to do so. All honor to these brave young men—Utica is proud of them, and when they return to their homes, and God grant that they may all return, they will be accorded a royal welcome. (Applause.)

The Glee Club sang "The Red, White and Blue" in excellent style.

President Proctor—The Oneida Historical Society feels under very great obligations to the gentleman who is to speak to you to-night, for the reason that he has come from New York, leaving regiments unprotected. He is commander of Lafayette post, which, as you know, has enlisted two regiments for this war. I take pleasure in introducing our own General Butterfield.

The veterans rose and greeted General Butterfield with three cheers. He said: President Proctor had not made me aware of this timely and interesting occasion in which we participate in the return of the flags. If he had, I might not have been present. For me it is something like a second christening. July 4, 1865, by designation of the governor and legislature, I was chosen to present to the governor and legislature the flags of the returned regiments. General Grant was present, and I made the address in front of the capitol at Albany. To come here and see some of the same flags returned seemed to me a little anomalous. I might have brought along a part of the address and read it here. But we had then no idea of the patriotism that would put up such a building here. It is very proper and right for the flags to be here, as it is a safe place and they will be an object lesson to the rising generation. I assure you I was as much touched by the sight of the flags as was Comrade Merriman. If you could have seen as I did and as did many of the comrades here, a row of dead men reaching from here to Genesee street bridge; they had only their names written on pieces of paper and pinned to the collars of their coats, and were then buried in a trench. If you had seen and known as I and these comrades did, of the men who gave their lives fearlessly, devotedly and gallantly for the old flag, you would feel touched as I was and as Comrade Merriman was, at the sight of these flags. (Applause.) Had I known what was coming, I should have prepared myself in an entirely different manner. Still, had I realized what was going on, I do not believe I should have stayed away.

Gen. Butterfield said that while these were stirring times, he realized that it was better for veterans who were reaching the line of three score and ten to consider the things that were rather than to think of participating in the events of to-day. It seems strange and difficult to realize it, especially as it seemed only a little while ago when the boys would look on a colonel who had reached the age of 50 and say: "There is an old duffer who ought to be at home."

Gen. Butterfield then launched out in stories of war and interesting reminiscences—anecdotes of the kind that soldiers tell about the camp fire. They were all the more interesting because he and many of his listeners had part in them. They were not in narrative form, but the incidental happenings, full of pith and point. Especially interesting were the stories of his personal dealings with the great men of the late war, like Grant and Lincoln. At the outset he related an anecdote told at his dinner table years ago by Gen. Winfield Scott. Then he showed how during the late war, Russia sympathized with the United States, and her attitude had much to do with preventing interference by England and France. He related an interview he had with the Confederate Gen. Pickett, in which Pickett said that up to the time Gen. Grant was placed in command he had no doubt the South would succeed. During the six days' fight in the Battle of the Wilderness, Grant demonstrated that he had staying qualities, and Pickett at once wrote his wife to send his negroes further south and sell them. He told an anecdote of Lincoln and Lord Lyons, and another of Lincoln and Seward, and the latter's decision in the Mason and Slidell case. Lincoln's readiness to meet an emergency was shown in a very interesting anecdote in which Gen. Hooker and Gen. Butterfield were concerned. Incidentally it showed how Gen. Gilmore was made a Major General, giving inside facts not generally known. Then followed another very interesting anecdote of Lincoln, his boy Thad., Gen. Sickles and the Princess Salm-Salm.

Referring to events of the present day Gen. Butterfield said: We are all looking to-day to see when the present war will end. We know of course that it will end when Sampson's fleet encounters and destroys the Spanish fleet.

Comparing the magnitude of the present war with that of the Civil War, he said: In this war 125,000 soldiers have been enlisted. The number of Union soldiers enlisted and re-enlisted during the civil war was 2,572,000. Of these 2,000,000 enlisted for three years, and 427,000 enlisted for one or two years. Putting it in another form there were 1.765 regiments of infantry, 270 regiments of cavalry, more than 900 batteries of artillery, and 671 ships of all kinds manned by 154,000 men. It took more men to man the ships then than have now been called out. During the civil war 364,116 died from wounds and disease, and this number did not include those who perished in Andersonville and Libby prisons. Those who sleep in unknown graves number over 150,000. The records show 5,825,000 entered at the hospitals during the war. These figures show the enormity of the struggle and its severity, but they give no figures on the other side. Is it any wonder that we cherish and love the veterans and stand by them? Their organization has no parallel in the history of the world. The money they have given to widows, their devotion to each other in illness, and the services performed by them is something unparalleled in the history of any of the armies of the world. I know Utica will give them the reception they deserve.

The present war will develop the same grand types of men and characters. When men read of Grant's address at Gettysburg they did not think much of it at the time. Just imagine such discipline as was shown by a sailor on board the Maine. He said to Capt. Sigsbee after saluting; "Sir, I have the honor to report that the ship is blown up and is sinking." (Applause.) Nothing in the history of warfare chronicles an incident in the line of discharge of duty more grand than this. You can stake your all on the United States navy. Utica had two good naval officers, Commodore Breeze and Commodore Mervin. Both, I believe, are buried in Forest Hill. I hope your society will place something on these walls in their memory.

The speaker described briefly Dewey's victory at Manilla and said: It made the tears roll down my cheeks when I read it. It was something for every American to be proud of. No matter what comes you can bet your bottom dollar on the American navy every time. (Applause.) We know that the climate of Cuba is terrible, and while we are anxious, we are equally confident that Sampson will be successful over the Spanish fleet if he has not already made that an accomplished fact. (Applause.) God bless our navy and our army. We know they will succeed. And God bless our President who has managed this war thus far with the greatest success. (Applause.)

On motion of David Jones, a vote of thanks was tendered to Gen. Butterfield for his very interesting address.

The exercises closed with the singing of "America." Then all the veterans came forward to shake the hand of the gallant soldier and distinguished general.

At six o'clock yesterday Gen. Butterfield was entertained at dinner by Mr. and Mrs. Thomas R. Proctor. The guests were: Gen. Daniel Butterfield, William M. Storrs, his brother-in-law; Col. C. H. Ballou, L. A. Jones, John Kohler, David Jones, Major James Miller, Gen Rufus Daggett, W. Stuart Walcott, J. H. Merriman, Arch B. Snow and Gen. C. W. Darling.

www.ingramcontent.com/pod-product-compliance
Lightning Source LLC
Chambersburg PA
CBHW020859160426
43192CB00007B/991